(HOLY) WHITEWATER

Reflections on the Spirituality of
Whitewater Kayaking

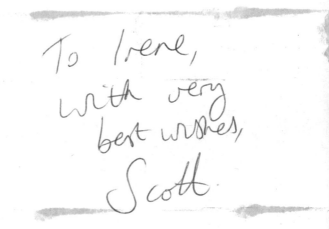

To Irene,
with very
best wishes,
Scott.

(HOLY) WHITEWATER

Reflections on the Spirituality of Whitewater Kayaking

Scott Burton

Astwood Publishing

© Scott Burton 2011

Published by Astwood Publishing Ltd
Astwood House
Carnoustie
Angus
DD7 6LW

Website: www.astwood.org.uk

ISBN 978-0-9566732-3-7

Cover design by Katelynne Kirk
Photograph by Shaun Ward
Website: www.shaunward.com

Whitewater kayaking, by definition, is a sport of risk and inherent hazard. The publisher and author of Holy Whitewater are not responsible for the application of any concepts suggested in this book.

Contents List

Acknowledgements   vii

Foreword   xi

Introduction   1

Journey on the River of Life   7

Riskiness OK   22

Be Strong and Courageous   39

Capsizing   54

River Rescue   64

Living Water   79

The River Guidebook   86

We All Need Eddies   99

Life in All Fullness   112

River Giver   114

Bibliography   121

About the Author   127

Acknowledgements

"Go, little book, and wish to all
Flowers in the garden, meat in the hall,
A bin of wine, a spice of wit,
A house with lawns enclosing it,
A living river by the door,
A nightingale in the sycamore!

Robert Louis Stevenson, Underwoods (1887)[1]

Writing a book is one of those things that I've hoped to accomplish for several years now. Like many others, I've had ideas for a few possible scripts, but never really found something quite as unique to write about as I believe the contents of this title are. It has been an interesting journey of discovery, learning about word counts, deadlines, publishing and marketing. I am, therefore, indebted to several people for the help I have had along the way.

One of the great helps was the publication, *Is There a Book in You?* by Alison Baverstock. You can imagine my pleasure when I read the following little paragraph to all virgin writers like myself. "They [each writer] may have to paddle in their own way, but perhaps not so much in their own lonely canoe. It helps to realise that there are lots of other people – and sensible, talented people at that – who are all in the same boat."[2] There's no question that

1 *The Oxford Library of Words and Phrases*, Volume I, p. 247
2 Baverstock, Alison, *Is There a Book in You?* p. X<insert p. no>

I've had many fellow 'paddlers' assisting this book into life and, so, for the support given, I offer the following words of gratitude.

My first and most precious paddling companion in this project, as in so many, is my wonderful, wonderful wife, Jill. "I'll love you dear, I'll love you till . . . the river jumps over the mountain" (W.H. Auden).[3] Then there are my two beautiful daughters, Eilidh and Sara, who not only put up with me using their laptops on a regular basis, but have also endured kayaking story after kayaking story. I'm the most blessed dad on the planet to have you two as my lassies.

The congregations where I've ministered in Kelty and Perth have taught me much more than I have ever taught anyone there. So, for the combined total of the education and support each member has offered, please accept my unending gratitude.

My friends at Perth Canoe Club are equally all stars in the lessons they have provided me on the water. Thanks for the laughs and all the times you've fished me out of the drink – especially Dave and Beaton! I'm sure if I've got something not quite right within these pages, you'll soon let me know!

The book cover has two wonderfully talented people to be grateful to: photographer Shaun Ward and graphic designer Katelynne Kirk. You two have been so patient with me in so many ways. Thank you so much! It looks fantastic!!

I'm indebted to Pat and Graham Giles for their editing of the draft of the text. Thanks for not using too much red pen, Pat!

---

3 *The Oxford Dictionary of Words and Phrases*, Volume I, p. 10

It is, too, my deep honour to have the foreword written by Professors Olive and John Drane, highly acclaimed international lecturers and best-selling authors in their own right. I cannot tell you how much I appreciate your prayerful encouragement and support.

Alan and Pamela Cairns at Astwood Publishing, you both gave me the confidence to believe this work actually is readable and worthy to be put into print. Thank you so much for all your enthusiasm, guidance and belief.

And finally, I thank the river giver, God himself, who has granted me the good health to write and paddle and live as I do. From source to sea, may my thanks to you be shown in the living out of my faith in loving action.

Scott Burton
Perth, on the Tay
August 2011

FOREWORD

Scott Burton is a man who loves adventure, and in this book he tells the story of how he became involved in one of the more extreme forms of adventure, whitewater kayaking. It's no surprise that he should have been tempted to make friends with the river Tay (Scotland's biggest river), as it's right on the doorstep of his church, and he has plenty of tales to tell about his struggles with the river in all its many phases and throughout the seasons; Sometimes calm, occasionally downright dangerous, and always unpredictable. But this is more than just the account of one man's battle with the constantly changing moods of nature: for Scott uses his kayaking adventures as a way of engaging with the journey we are all engaged in, as we try to get from one day to the next while living life in ways that will bring meaning to ourselves and that will be nurturing to other people.

When you think about it, the fast changing speed of the river, and the sort of skills needed to navigate it safely – whether you're speeding along on the crest of a wave or capsizing in a whirlpool – is remarkably similar to everyday life. Just when you think you're in control of it all, something unexpected hits you round the next corner and we so easily end up in a whirlpool, being sucked under by forces that threaten to overwhelm us. Lessons learned in the river have much to teach us. As Scott shares his stories, he is in turn funny, fearful and insightful – and always conversational. In the process, he introduces readers to a veritable galaxy of spiritual and sporting characters who have much to contribute to our own personal stories. Where else would you find kayaking champions like Ken Whiting and Franco Ferrero in conversation with Rob Bell and the Pope – or renegade Dominican Matthew Fox alongside Dominican master Timothy Radcliffe, not to mention Derren Brown, Bear Grylls, and Richard Dawkins?

Scott does what all the best storytellers do, sharing just enough of his own personal struggles to entice you to want to know more. But this is no miserable introspective account. Throughout it all, Scott's deep Christian faith shines through in a way that joins up all these different aspects of his life. There are no simplistic answers on offer here, just a load of really good questions and an invitation to join him on the journey, following Jesus in ways that make sense in today's unpredictable world.

After reading this, you may never even be tempted to try kayaking for yourself – but the river will never look the same again.

John Drane
Olive Fleming Drane

INTRODUCTION

"Recreation can lead to new ways of seeing and new patterns of behaviour."

Archie Smith Jr, *Navigating the Deep River*, p. 145

Imagine yourself, in a plastic kayak, hurtling down the rapids of a strong river near your home. The rain has not ceased for days. The water levels are high. Most people have opted to stay indoors rather than venture outside only to get soaked to the skin. You, though, *want* to get wet! You're thanking God for the seventy-two hours worth of incessant downpour! You can't get to the river quickly enough to experience one of the most exhilarating, natural roller-coaster rides full of wave trains, waterfalls, undercurrents and whirlpools.

After un-strapping your boat from the roof of your car and changing into your purpose-made gear (including, of course, the critical safety equipment of helmet and buoyancy aid) you squeeze inside the cockpit of the vessel that will help you carve through the waters. Having secured your spray deck to keep the river out of the boat and the boat out on the river, you seal-launch down the riverbank into the millions of gallons of H_2O pouring past at colossal volume. You're wet instantly and, already, now that you've emerged from below the river's surface, you have had to brace to avoid capsize.

To begin with a short, gentle paddle on relatively calm water is all that needs to be negotiated. With the crescendo of whitewater more and more audible just yards away, however, you soon find yourself right in the middle of one of several rapid sections on the river's course. The cold water, undulating with the rocks below, catches your breath as it drenches your face relentlessly. Your heart is racing. You're mind is working overtime as you endeavour to follow the best line. In fact, your whole body, using muscles you never realised you had, is straining to put together all the skills you've learnt about paddling, bracing, edging and (hoping you manage when required) Eskimo-rolling back upright. You'll never do it – control the river, that is. You're at its constant mercy, but the challenge is in attempting to at least control yourself on this remarkable and powerful highway of nature.

All the time, you only have around 5 mm of plastic between your rear and the fast-flowing torrent beneath you. There are rocks all around with the potential of cracking open your skull or at least shattering an elbow or two. The flow is furious. Eddy lines and boils are persistent in pushing you one way and then the next. It's exciting and demanding simultaneously, which is, of course, what drove you to launch out in the first place. So you continue on, a mere speck on the surface of the enormity of the mighty flow. In earnest, you seek to stay vigilant for ever-present boulders and strainers and holes, along with any number of other life-threatening dangers. This is an environment that commands respect. So maintain your balance, avoid capsize and, above all, try your hardest not to end up swimming in the chill of the billowing river.

Such is my brief and very, very inadequate word-picture of what it is to enjoy the thrill of whitewater kayaking. It is, though, an attempted description of the realities of such a trip by a Church of Scotland minister (a paddling padre if you will) who has only discovered this magnificent sport in his years of middle age.

And, oh, what a buzz the *real* trip is! Words truly cannot convey! In these middle years of life I am finding that this wonderful form of recreation has also become a brilliant teacher to me. It is as a paddler and as a pastor I have been learning much that there is in common with this real river and the river we call life. Kayaking down the water that flows within the banks has led me to a new way of seeing things and a new place for seeing new lessons in things already familiar. I'm writing here about the spirituality of the river and how I've found it help me, as a Christian, in my personal and professional journey with God. Hopefully, there might be something here to help you in your journey too.

In his book, *Navigating the Deep River*, professor of pastoral psychology, Archie Smith Jr says that, "The river metaphor provides an imaginative way to talk about spirituality".[4] It certainly does! The river has a source; so does life. The river has a path to find and follow; so do we. The river has an end point where it meets the vast unknown of the deep, deep ocean; such is our common humanity as we, one day, go far beyond this world out into the mysteries of eternity.

You get the point, I'm sure. Here I shall be writing about one of the great guidebooks for living, the Bible, alongside the river guidebooks so helpful for paddling. When I address the need for time out to worship or pray or con-

---

4 Smith Jr, Archie, *Navigating the Deep River*, p. 145

template, as every Christian tradition has done for two millennia, I'll marry such concepts to the need everyone in a kayak has to find quiet, safe, still eddies amidst the mad rush of strong currents. And when I mention evangelistic zeal and passion, or the desire to convert people to a new way of living "life in all fullness" (John 10:10), I'll mention. . . an expert kayaker! Eh?

In his superb introductory book on the subject of the various forms of kayaking, world-champion, Ken Whiting, declares, "Let the truth be known that kayaking is PURE FUN!"[5] That's quite an evangelical statement right there really, "let the truth be known". Boy, is Ken on the ball to proclaim his particular gospel with such zeal! Kayaking *is* pure fun!

Knowing that the "fun" part is not terribly true to my Calvinistic roots, in these pages I'll address the spirituality in the sport (though, since I'm not very true to my Calvinistic roots generally, I hope we will also have at least a little fun along the way). As one who is more used to speaking about the guy who walked on the water than addressing how all of us can learn to surf on it, I'll stick to what I know best. I'll aim, nevertheless, to contrast this with what I've been learning about kayaking as thrilling, scary, challenging, confidence-building, physical and spiritual fun. Yes, *spiritual* fun.

To quote Ken Whiting once more: "Whitewater kayaking is much more than just a physical activity. . . . It will in myriad ways challenge you, strengthen you, reward you, connect you, mystify you, and, most importantly, free you".[6] Challenge. Strengthen. Reward. Connect. Mystify. Free. These can all be very spiritual words, and I hope

---

5 Whiting, Ken, *Whitewater Kayaking – The Ultimate Guide*, p. viii
6 Whiting, Ken, *Whitewater Kayaking – The Ultimate Guide*, p. ix

to elaborate upon them in different ways. There is absolutely no doubt in my mind that careering down a river is a wonderful dimension of this 'fullness of life' that my boss came to give physically *and* spiritually!

According to another expert, world-class kayaker, Doug Ammons (who you shall find I quote often here), the physical and the spiritual really do merge into one. He says, "The reason we are even on the river in a kayak in the first place is that it is the most fun, wildest, greatest sport in the world. . . . It is as if you took the best amusement park in the world, joined it with the most beautiful surroundings, and then got on intimate terms with God about how he runs the whole show. It's exciting and fascinating, humbling and inspiring. In a word, it's a celebration of life".[7] I couldn't have said it better! Life in all fullness.

Simply put, then, the substance of this book's message is that kayaking is good for the soul. Whitewater kayaking, which is my main area of involvement, is a uniquely invigorating, life-enhancing, pure adrenalin-pumping adventure from start to finish. Irrespective of which particular river you happen to be on, this sport can teach about creation, our self, life, handling fear and failure and, no less, the ever real and abundant need for rescue or salvation.

In many ways, what I write is nothing new! As is written in *Wildwater* by Lito Tejada-Flores, "Rivers themselves have always been objects of power and reverence, inspiring symbol and myth".[8] Maybe so, but it is new to me and, I hope you can tell, I write of what has become a passion; a passion of which I am now a complete convert, and disciple. I'd be delighted, then, if you will continue a

---

7 Ammons, Doug, *Whitewater Philosophy*, p. 136

8 Tejada-Flores, Lito, *Wildwater*, Sierra Club Books, San Francisco, 1978, p. 9

while longer with me as I contemplate the sheer pleasure of running a river and learning from it along the way.

Scott Burton
Perth, on the Tay, 2011

JOURNEY ON THE
RIVER OF LIFE

"Each one of us has a particular river to ride."

Larry Christenson, *Ride the River*, p. 22

"Living is moving; time is a live creek."

Annie Dillard, *Pilgrim at Tinker Creek*, p. 82

Towering over the longest river in Scotland – the Tay – is the tallest man-made pinnacle in beautiful Perth: St. Matthew's Church of Scotland, in the heart of the ancient capital city. This happens to be the church building, with its 212 foot spire, built by architect John Honeyman in 1871, which houses the congregation of wonderful people whom I am privileged to serve as their full time minister.

You need to see the view for yourself if you haven't already. In fact, you can, easily. The image of St. Matthew's by the Tay is on nearly every website, postcard, tourist brochure and shortbread tin associated with the fair city of Perth. In fact, in many ways this is *the* image of Perth, and I love it just as much as many others, self-evidently, do.

Yet, this book is inspired by the fact that I have seen both the church and the river from quite different angles than most. As the minister I see the river from the front door of the church. As a kayaker I see the front door of the church from the river. What this unique ecclesiastical and water-sport blend does, is stir my mind with all sorts of meandering thoughts about the spirituality of the river.

I am seeing life literally and metaphorically from a very new perspective these days. I believe that the very creator of the earth and sea and the river and land would approve, entirely, of my new hobby. In fact I would ask the question W.W.J.P.? "What Would Jesus Paddle?" The answer is, I think, anything that would help him get on the water and delight in the pleasures of holy whitewater because, as Doug Ammons declares in *Whitewater Philosophy*, "All outward journeys should also be inward journeys".[9]

In July 2007 I had the fabulous experience of exchanging pulpits with a colleague in the Presbyterian Church, USA. For three weeks, the Reverend Janelle Tibbets-Vaughan came to Perth, Scotland, to preach to and pastor my congregation. I had the equally great pleasure of going to Encino, Los Angeles, where Janelle is the associate pastor.

Encino is where the family of the late king of pop, Michael Jackson, live. Though I never had the chance to meet any of the Jacksons, or even see where their home was, I did have a far greater privilege in my eyes: to meet the legendary coach, John Wooden. Sadly, John died in June 2010 at the age of 99.

In Scotland, unfortunately, very few people will have heard of John Wooden as he was a basketball coach, which is pretty much a minority sport in the UK. In the USA, though, basketball is massive, and so was John Wooden (even if he was, like me, short in physical stature). Coach Wooden took the University of California Los Angeles

---

9 Ammons, Doug, *Whitewater Philosophy*, p. ii

basketball team to 10 March Madness national championships in 12 years; 7 national championships in a row; an
88 game winning streak; and four 'perfect' seasons. He is
quite simply the most accomplished, yet humble, man I
think I have ever met!

I'm sure you're asking why I am recounting all this in
a book about kayaking and the river and spirituality. It's
simply because Coach John Wooden had realised and
shared for a long time the lesson of life that, "Basketball
is about more than basketball".[10] Well, kayaking is about
more than kayaking too!

Aged 97, when I went to his apartment because of his
commitment to Christ and his involvement with First
Presbyterian Church, Encino, Coach Wooden sat and
regaled me with poetry, conversed with complete clarity of
thought and spoke in ever such humble tones of his many,
many achievements. As a result of that privileged time, I
know John believed that who we are has a very strong
impact upon what we take to any sport, and equally, what
the sport is can have a very strong impact upon who we
are. This is definitely true with kayaking. As much as the
sheer thrill of the whitewater could be reason enough to
get involved, there are multiple other factors that we can
take from this pastime and much that we can take to it by
the nature of who we are.

In an increasingly obese society, kayaking can be about
physical exercise.

In constantly expanding suburbia, kayaking can be
about getting back to nature.

In a world that is more and more paranoid about security, kayaking can be about getting out of our comfort zone
to enjoy our vulnerability.

---

10 Wooden, John and Jamison, Steve, *Wooden on Leadership*, p. 64

In a world of stress and competing demands, kayaking can be about freedom and liberation from all that weighs us down.

In our increasingly secular world which squeezes out our innate spirituality, kayaking can be about being at one with creation and, indeed, the Creator.

Inevitably, you see, we kayak on our external journey down a river[11] (after you have, hopefully, taken at least a few weeks coaching in a local swimming pool or on a flat water loch!). The comparisons to this sport and spirituality, then, really ought not to be of any surprise, for rivers have been associated with God, faith and spirituality for centuries and in many different cultures.

In his book, *One River, Many Wells*, Matthew Fox has compiled a collection of wonderful quotes from many faith traditions:

From the aboriginal faith community:

"I am a child of the Dreamtime People
Part of the land, like the gnarled gumtree
I am the river, softly singing
Chanting our songs on the way to the sea."[12]

From the Native American Peoples:

"We should understand well that all things are the
work of the Great Spirit. We should know that he is
within all things; the trees the grasses the rivers. . ."[13]

---

11 There is, of course, surf and sea kayaking and kayaking across lochs and lakes. I understand this well. My focus is upon the whitewater elements sport and what we can learn from this particular discipline.

12 Quoted in *One River, Many Wells* by Matthew Fox, p. 182

13 Quoted in *One River, Many Wells* by Matthew Fox, p. 48

From the Hindu mystic:

"The worship of the different religions, which are like so many small streams, move together to meet God, who is like the ocean."[14]

In my own faith tradition of Christianity, the Bible begins and ends with rivers. The first book of the Bible, Genesis (Chapter 2:10), talks of the garden of Eden with the stream running through it and the four rivers that flow beyond. Some 65 books of the Bible later, all the way to Revelation (Chapter 22:1) it talks about the River of Life. In between this there will be few of us who would not be aware of the song in the book of Psalms that begins, "By the Rivers of Babylon" (made even more famous, of course by the 70s group, Boney M). I trust, too, that many will recall the fact that the baby Moses was placed in a basket of reeds and was hidden on the Nile River and that Jesus himself was baptised in the River Jordan.

The Old Testament prophet, Amos, declared, "Let justice flow like rivers, and righteousness like a never-failing stream" (Amos 5:24) and, again, the Psalmist (Psalm 1) helpfully says that we will be like a tree planted by a stream, healthy in ourselves, if we root ourselves in God's teachings. In John's Gospel in the New Testament, Jesus even talked about himself being the living water, as opposed to the stagnant water in cisterns that people had to often rely upon in the sweltering heat of ancient Palestine. Here J.C. was using the symbolism of refreshing, flowing, life-giving water about himself as he brings nourishment and vitality to the soul.

In the book, *Love Wins*, Rob Bell makes the point that, "In the Genesis poem that begins the Bible, life is a pulsing,

---

14 Quoted in *One River, Many Wells* by Matthew Fox, p. 418

progressing, evolving, dynamic reality in which tomorrow will not be a repeat of today, because things are, at the most fundamental level of existence, going somewhere". [15] Simply change the word 'life' for 'the river' in Bell's quote and it is easy to see the similarities between the two!

The metaphorical idea of life being like a river, a moving body of water, is very well known. It changes as it goes on its journey and it is, indeed, changed by its journey as it goes. So, the comparison between a river and our personal journey of life is really very profound! As the river flows constantly, so does our allotted time on earth. Larry Christenson, in his book *Ride the River*, makes this very clear when he declares, "Every person has a river to ride. . . . God has laid out a plan for your life, a river that you are to follow. . . . But you will discover the actual plan for your life only as you make the journey. . . . God's command is plain, and it covers your life from beginning to end: you are to Ride the River".[16]

No two human beings ever ride the river the same way though, or experience the same things. You and I are utterly, utterly unique; that is one of the amazing things about our human condition. Out of a present world population of over six and a half billion souls, no one (did you get that? No one!!) will ever be like you or me, and you and I will never come close to the life of anyone else. This is where our spirituality kicks in. Who am I? Why am I here? What is my life's purpose? These are questions we all ask and all long to find an answer to. Seek and you shall find!

Again, this is one of the wonderful things about the religious tradition to which I happen to belong. There is no one, solitary, way of believing in Jesus. As Rob Bell, again, says in his book *Love Wins*, "That's the beauty of

---

15 Bell, Rob, *Love Wins*, p. 44
16 Christenson, Larry, *Ride the River*, p. 30

the historic, orthodox Christian faith. It's a deep, wide, diverse stream that's been flowing for thousands of years, carrying a staggering variety of voices, perspectives, and experiences". [17]

Blaise Pascal said that "Rivers are roads that move and carry us whither we wish to go".[18] The ancient Greek philosopher, Heraclitus of Ephesus, also said that, "You can't step into the same river twice".[19] And so, every quote given, every sage mentioned, takes us deeper and deeper into an understanding that our lives are just like the waters that carry a kayaker along. There really is something very deep about a river, deeper than even the riverbed below the flowing current.

In *Your Spiritual Journey – A Guide to the River of Life*, Ruth White begins by asking her readers to "Visualise a river, flowing from its source to the sea. Imagine it as the river of your life".[20] I suppose I am asking us all to do something similar here. It is, after all, a great concept that withstands the test of time, assisting us to reflect on how we have such a remarkable place upon this planet and to ponder from where we have come and to where we are going.

Reflecting on the river as we can, literally and metaphorically, we shall see that, little by little, we have all grown through infancy to childhood to teenage years to adulthood. We've changed with every paddle stroke along the way. As we go, the imagery reminds us that we have each faced times of peace, like the calm water sections, and times

---

17 Bell, Rob, *Love Wins*, p. xi

18 Quoted in *Peace like a River* by Donney Finley, p. 6

19 Partington, Angela (Ed), *The Oxford Library of Words and Phrases: Quotations. Volume I*, 2nd Edition, p. 118

20 White, Ruth, *Your Spiritual Journey – A Guide to the River of Life*, p. 7

of confusion and rage like the varying grades of rapid that demand so much of our energy. Carry the metaphor further and we can contemplate what have been the contributing factors to the people and personalities we have become, in a similar way to the tributary rivers that flow into the main body of water making it what *it* has become.

I think that I think like this because I'm a church minister. I can hardly help it. It's the way us clergy are wired. We get all heavy and holy even when we should be just having a laugh. But then, what am I to do? Not only does the mighty river Tay flow right past the doorstep of St. Matthew's Church where I preach each week, but I also regularly meet people whose lives are as dynamic and changeable as those great waters.

In the tears of a husband who grieves his wife's loss in their golden anniversary year, or the anguish of a mother and father who have lost their child before his first birthday, I see the doubts and fears and rage that such rapid sections of life's river bring. In the serene calm upon the face of the lady of faith who is on a hospital bed, awaiting radical surgery, I contrast the paddle I can have on the gentle sections of rivers before the many obstacles ahead create all sorts of challenges and trials.

In the teenager asking me to pray for them as they approach their exams, or the business woman worried about the recession, or in the face of the baby I have in my arms to be baptised, I see so many comparisons to the river. There's the fear I have of the tests that the river brings me, the worry about being capsized without the ability to roll right side up again, and there's the joy at simply being on and in the water that I relish time after time. "The fluid nature of water is integral to understanding our journey",[21]

---

21 Susan, Saint Sing, *Spirituality of Sport*, p. 14

comments the author of *Spirituality of Sport* Susan Saint Sing. How right she is. Life has a particular flow to it and each life, like each river, is really rather unique. Welsh comedian Griff Rhys Jones has also said, within the marvellous and illuminating pages of his book *Rivers*, "It's a spiritual thing, flowing water".[22]

It really is a spiritual thing, flowing water. I find God there and he finds me. The river, as much as being a place of fun and excitement, is also a place of prayer and devotion. Again, Ruth White, although coming from a very different perspective of spirituality than me, gets it right when she says,

"We all tend to live a little in the past and/or future as well as in the present. Mighty rivers flow to the sea. Do the droplets emerging from the source know their destiny? Are those same droplets contained in the flow which we watch as we stand at the river's edge? Have they been changed as a result of their journey thus far? Will they change again as they move on? Will a continuing essence be carried from the source to the sea?"[23]

This is all deep stuff, if you'll pardon the pun! That's okay though. Kayakers aren't frightened of going deep. In fact, the deeper the better when you're taking your last vital paddle stroke before plummeting over some large waterfall or another! "The boils that sometimes form at the bottom of a waterfall are just what a kayaker wants." says extreme kayaker, Tao Berman: "They soften the entry like a pillow".[24] This book is trying to act like those boils,

---

22 Jones, Griff Rhys, *Rivers – A Voyage into the Heart of Britain*, p. 154

23 White, Ruth, *Your Spiritual Journey – A Guide to the River of Life*, p. 8

24 Berman, Tao, *Going Vertical – The Life of an Extreme Kayaker*, p. 125

softening the entry into our personal consideration of our spirituality. If we're brave enough to face such literal depth, why should we be in any way anxious about going deep in philosophical and theological thought too?

These are extreme questions, but then, whitewater kayaking is an extreme sport. The profundities I'm encouraging us to enter into are not dissimilar to the pondering that most of us will find ourselves involved in at some stage or another anyway. We all have thoughts about our existence, the direction of our lives and the meaning or purpose of why we are here at all. Though we might be fooled into believing all the hype that 'science has replaced the need for religion' or that 'no one believes in the need for faith anymore', the truth is that no one can be completely sure of anything. I can't even be sure that we can't be sure of anything!

Still, I do share with the Christian population throughout the world a belief that life does have a purpose, that God is the source of our being, that he is with us to help in times of difficulty and that, though tragedy does of course still come, he loves us and longs for us to love him in return.

Personally, I can map much of this belief back to my upbringing, baptised and raised in a church on the south side of the city of Glasgow as I was. Through my childhood I happily soaked in the stories of Noah and the ark, Jonah and the whale, and Jesus calming the storm. Equally, though, I am conscious of my departure from all things faith related. I remember, with fondness actually, the friends I used to join on a Saturday night, causing trouble on street corners and getting drunk within the local park. I remember, too, a silly time when I was charged by the police with a breach of the peace and possession of offensive weapons and was fined £200 in Paisley Sheriff Court for my nonsensical behaviour. Still, to this day, if I am checked out by Disclosure Scotland for safeguarding purposes in any work with children that I do, my form reads thus: "Convictions – Breach of Peace and Prevention of Crime Act 1953 Section 1(1)"

These were periods when the river of my particular life was taking new turns, and still more were to come along the way when I decided that I needed or hankered after personal faith again. The further I was getting away from the Source of my existence, the more contaminated my personal waters were becoming. That's when and why I made the conscious decision to be part of the church once more, and from there on I can honestly say that life has never been the same again. It has been a fabulous adventure of meeting many people, travelling many places, entering many situations of celebration and tribulation and simply trying to follow the best life coach I have found out there: Jesus Christ.

That's the way it is for us all, isn't it? "Life is a fluid realm",[25] as Leonard Sweet puts it in *Soul Tsunami*. We experience things, make decisions, have others influence us and we end up just where we are, just as we are. In the same way as there is not one river in the world that is merely pure, crystal-clear, sparkling water, so our lives are a combination of our inherent, God-given goodness and purity along with the various forms of debris and silt that is mixed in along the way. We look for guidance from many different sources and we move along accordingly, sometimes right side up with the warmth of the sun on our face, other times capsizing with the chill of the waters shocking us to the core.

Like any river running through any part of our planet, our beliefs and thinking will change throughout the twists

---

25 Sweet, Leonard, *Soul Tsunami*, p. 81

and turns, depending where we are on life's journey, what input we have had, the obstacles that we encounter and the times in which we find ourselves. Even the evangelistic atheist, Richard Dawkins, at this stage of *his* journey, after all the studying he has done, the debating he has been involved in, and the books he has written can only conclusively say that, "God, though not technically disprovable, is very, very improbable indeed".[26] Dawkins is not *completely* sure either!

Of course, as a minister of the Kirk, I don't agree with Professor Dawkins' conclusion about the improbability of a deity who is the source of all that is. I rather think that God is closer than any of us may think, and I echo what the vicar at the Holy Isle has said in one of his many beautiful prayers: "The sun and stars, the valleys and hills, the rivers and the lakes, all disclose your presence".[27] There's spirituality to the river.

I don't wish to pretend, however, that this journey of faith is easy or always very pretty. I have found that it is often, very often, far, far from that! In fact, it is because I have found whitewater kayaking so challenging in many ways that I can relate it to my life as a Christian. I've capsized more times than I care to mention and swum on more occasions than my ego will allow me to declare. My kayaking helmet has some small, and some not-so-small, scratches on it from underwater encounters with rocks in the Rivers Tay, Tummel and Etive. I can very sincerely say, therefore, that I relate entirely to what American pastor and author Eugene Peterson says in his helpful book, *The Journey*: "No sooner have we plunged, expectantly and enthusiastically, into the river of Christian faith than we

26 Dawkins, Richard, *The God Delusion*, p. 136.
27 Adam, David, *The Rhythm of Life*, p. 30

get our noses full of water and come up coughing and choking".[28] If truth be told, I find it all rather amusing that many church folk seem to expect life to be otherwise.

If anyone tells you that becoming a Christian will make your life perfect, trouble-free and lovely, please don't believe a word of it. It just is not true. The rocks and rapids may well come at any one of us unyieldingly. We *will* be capsized many times over and we won't always manage to roll back up. There will be times when we, quite frankly, cannot cope on our own and we'll need the help of others. Indeed, we may end up swimming through section after section of life's river, struggling to catch our breath, desperately longing for the bank, living in great fear, cold, bruised and even laughed at from others who aren't, for whatever reason, finding that section quite as demanding.

Does that all sound too negative? It is not meant to. I'm just trying to be realistic and honest. Just as kayaking has many different peaks and troughs, so does life too, whether we are Christians or not. What I find in my journey with God is that, irrespective of the difficult sections of life, there is always a strength that comes from knowing you are not travelling alone. I love life all the more, in fact, for the variety of triumphs and the tribulations. Sure, the hard times are never easy, but they make the good times even more fabulous. It is life in all fullness Christ promised, not life in all blandness.

The longer I live upon this mysterious planet, the more I love the life it offers. The more I have kayaked on whitewater and flat water, the more I have fallen in love with the river. I find it becoming more and more of a teacher to me in terms of who I am and what my faith is about. As Edgar Lee Masters said in a beautiful piece of prose, I have been

---

28 Peterson, Eugene, *The Journey*, p. 24

wonderfully surprised to find that, "The soul of the river had entered my soul. . ."[29]

Maria Coffey says the same kind of thing in her book about the spiritual lives of extreme athletes, *Explorers of the Infinite*: "I was part of the river now and she was part of me".[30] Maria was sharing her own story of the time she and her husband kayaked down the river Ganges in India, dissuaded to do so by everyone she met. However, they proceeded to paddle onward and face what they would encounter along the way. That journey forced Maria to flee from a man chasing her and her partner along the bank with his rifle raised, paddle around floating human bodies that had been given over to the water that is believed to be sacred by locals, and ever so quietly drift by drunken bandits in the darkness of the night for fear of their lives. Yet, in her own words, "Our voyage along the river had turned me inside out, challenged me on every level".[31]

Maria also quotes Sam Drevo, a professional kayaker from Oregon. He'd been paddling through a very demanding section of the Rio Jimenoa in the Dominican Republic when he came to a calm section in a high, constricted gorge with very tranquil waters. The stark contrast to the raging rapids he had just come through became a spiritual moment when, he says, "It was like I reached a place where clarity and intuition and focus all came together to bring me to a higher level of consciousness – a level where I was no longer me; I was part of the river".[32]

All this said, however, I would not presume to impose such river spirituality upon others for whom such a notion might be jarring or seemingly irrelevant in its imagery. All

---

29 Quoted in *Peace Like a River* by Donny Finley, p. 13
30 Coffey, Maria, *Explorers of the Infinite*, p. 102
31 Coffey, Maria, *Explorers of the Infinite*, p. 103
32 Quoted in Coffey, Maria, *Explorers of the Infinite*, p. 57

I do here is say that there is something special about these moving channels of water for me, and I sense that there is a spiritual throw-line that can be tossed to us anytime we need it. God in Christ is my daily 'paddling' partner. "I will never leave you or forsake you" (Hebrews 13:5). Reach out and grab. "Be assured I am with you always" (Matthew 28:20). He really has got the whole world in his hands! "Do not be afraid" (Mark 6:50).

Anyway, isn't all this thrashing about in the river, the water-swallowing, the rock bashing and the breath-holding all part of the great adventure? Of course it is! Kayaking is about more than kayaking, so paddle your own boat and get onto the water for the ride of your life.

Riskiness OK

"*God did not give us a spirit of timidity.*"

2 Timothy 1:17

"*Life would be boring without risk.*"

Tao Berman, *Going Vertical – The Life of an Extreme Kayaker*, p. 134

As a Church of Scotland minister I am, by default, moderator of my congregation's leadership team. Within the Presbyterian system of Church government, whether in Scotland or elsewhere, this local body is known as the Kirk Session.

Over recent years, Kirk Sessions have sometimes got a bit of a bad name for themselves. The way they work can be stereotypically slow, cautious and (ouch) boring. Many times colleagues of mine will talk of their frustrations and of how tired of the Session they have become. Such weariness is because of the general lack of willingness that can be evident in trying out new things, moving with the times and changing much of the way that the church operates from within, particularly Victorian traditions to 21st Century practices.

I have known such frustrations too. Man, have I some-times wanted to create a Kirk Session bypass! However, generally, I have been very blessed to work with two excellent Kirk Sessions: firstly when I was minister in the ex-coal-mining community of Kelty in West Fife, and secondly in the city centre charge of St. Matthew's, Perth where I currently am located. Both of these Kirk Sessions seem to have understood well that, to be a Christian and, more than this, to be a Christian leader, is to be someone willing and able to take risks.

Over the years I have marvelled at how my fellow Kirk Session members, though filled with reservation and doubts, have bravely agreed to come with me into new and strange territory, like leading some of our church services in a local bar, opening the church doors late on a Saturday night for worship, or investing hundreds of thousands of pounds in building projects that I've prompted as being worthy of our resources. Still, it is a risky business, change, and most of us don't like it very much.

Author Dan Gardner, who published a book simply called *Risk*, summarises things perfectly: "In a sentence: We are the healthiest, wealthiest, and longest-lived people in history. And we are incredibly afraid. This is one of the greatest paradoxes of our time".[33]

We can also quote our whitewater philosopher friend, Doug Ammons when he says, "From what I've seen, most of the fears kayakers feel are unrealistic – we're fearful even when in reality we are quite safe". [34]

And to drive the point home still further from a man of God, similar sentiment is highlighted by Dominican Friar, Timothy Radcliffe, in his book *What is the Point of Being a Christian*? He states, "In many ways we are safer than

33 Gardner, Dan, *Risk*, p. 11
34 Ammons, Doug, *Whitewater Philosophy*, p. 140

our ancestors. At least in the West we are more protected from illness, violence and poverty. And yet we are afraid". Radcliffe then offers the encouragement of the consistently courageous Pope John Paul II that every kayaker will appreciate well: "*Novo millennio ineunte*. The phrase is: 'Put out into the deep'".[35]

Helping others rise to the challenge of risk-taking – putting out into the deep – is a big issue in the local church. For me, there have been several influences upon me in this regard. One of the greatest encouragers has been the Revd Peter Neilson, my former minister when I was growing up in Glasgow. Peter is a leading light in the Church of Scotland and an author of an incredibly influential report to our General Assembly called *Church Without Walls*. In that report Peter writes, "The love of security is addictive. It will take courage and commitment to break that addiction".[36] How right he is! Also, in a book that Peter has written called *Church on the Move,* he says, "The river of the Spirit is running in new places in our culture, and old patterns of church are being by-passed. Our task is to discern where the river of God is running and to form new patterns of church there".[37]

Rivers do change their course over time – that's a matter of fact. Churches, as with any other organisation, institution or body of people, will also develop and redevelop throughout their lifetime. In the church, it somehow feels harder though, especially when the transitions we have seen around us in wider society have come at the incredible, unprecedented speed that they have in the past century or

---

35 Radcliffe, Timothy O.P., *What is the Point of Being a Christian?*, Burns and Oates, London 2006, p. 70, 71.

36 Reports to the General Assembly of the Church of Scotland 2001, p. 36/9

37 Neilson, Peter, *Church on the Move*, p. 75

so. It is as if the 'River of God', as Peter Neilson calls it, has entered a frenetic stretch within living memory, and many of those who have been used to paddling through calmer waters now are very fearful of the rapids that we are encountering and needing to navigate. It *is* risky and it *is* daunting and it *is* scary. But Christianity is not a fear-filled faith, so risk-taking really ought to come naturally!

This is why I lead morning worship in St. Matthews at the traditional time of 11am and why I also lead an alternative worship service called Sanctuary First, which runs from 8–10pm on a Saturday night. On Christmas Eve, much to the interest of local, national and international news agencies, we also lead our Christmas watchnight service in the bar next door. We set ourselves up in the early evening, then go through around 10pm to mix with those gathered there (around 300–400 folk). We lead a half-hour service of carol singing and prayers from 11:30pm into Christmas morning with people who will likely have a beer or a gin and tonic in their hands.

Actually, I conduct the service whilst sipping on a specially created local beer called St. Matthew's ale, created by our local Inveralmond Brewery to help raise funds for repairs to our massive 212 foot spire. That itself has been a strong bone of contention leading to a live interview on BBC Radio Scotland to defend our action. However, given that Trappist monks have been brewing fine ales for centuries, the acceptance of a local brewer's support is not action that I am going to shy away from easily as if our 21st century actions are somehow new and unprecedented.

Undoubtedly, though, such activity is risky! But that's where I easily compare what I do as a minister to what I do on the water. Ronald Cameron, author of *Tall Stories* – the biography about Scotland's late, inspirational, pioneering kayaker, Andy Jackson – says it well: "In whitewater kayaking we get used to weighing potential thrills versus potential spills. It's good; it's healthy. It keeps us on the edge, keeps life exciting and just sometimes it catches us out".[38] I would much prefer to be in the risky environment of a pub nearing closing time where people heckle me than in the safe environment of a church where my respectful, attentive congregation will most likely say, "Nice service, minister" irrespective of whether it really was or not. It's not that I don't enjoy quieter more attentive congregations. I do. But just as on the river, it is good to paddle choppier waters as well as the calm.

At St. Matthew's, we've had a few of our church members leave our congregation over these Christmas Eve services in the pub. We also had anonymous complaints submitted to newspapers about our activities. Such facts are never easy to handle as the minister. It hurts to have parts of the church body decide to break away and other parts misunderstand or speak in derogatory tones about the work we are engaged in. That said, I am constantly encouraged by the fact that Jesus himself was criticised and misunderstood during his earthly ministry. He could have turned water into pomegranate juice, but he chose to change it into wine instead. He could have preached in the relatively safer confines of the temple or synagogue, but he chose to share his teaching on the streets and hillside, as well as in the homes of many of society's 'outcasts'.

I am always sorry that there are some who feel so strongly that they feel the need to cut their ties with the congregation where I minister – even if they are leaving to go and worship elsewhere. It does, however, cause me greater anxiety to know there are people outside of the church community who think that they are not welcomed

---

38 Cameron, Ronald, *Tall Stories*, p. 49.

by God or that the church is not interested in them, so much so that they will not come inside our imposing buildings. That's why I take the risks that I do – and indeed why Jesus himself took the risk of the incarnation, which is what Christmas is, actually, all about! He wanted to be with us, God with us in the world, and I'm happy to be where he is, whether inside a church building or inside a bar or on the river.

A colleague, former minister of Riverside Church in Perth, Revd Fred Drummond, now the General Secretary of the Scottish Evangelical Alliance, agrees: "Living out faith in the midst of people who have never considered that Jesus may make a difference to them will not be easy, but it is part of the incarnational ministry of the church. It is what we are called to".[39]

In his book, *The River Within*, Jeff Imbach makes the same point: "Living passionately is about living wide and living deep. To live passionately as a Christian is to live wide – wide open to God and wide open to life. . . . It calls us to trust that God will be with us through the many twists and turns of the journey of life. It challenges us to risk letting go of everything that detracts from the free flowing of God's life in us".[40]

Absolutely! The God of Christianity is a God of action. He does not call us to live a narrow, shallow, easy-discipleship! He calls us to get out there onto the river, even into the whitewater sections that will get our hearts pumping and adrenalin flowing through our veins. This is great news for the Church!

Once, when I was playing around with an anagram-making program on the internet, I decided I would type in the words 'Kirk' and 'Session' to see what came up. Bizarre

39 Drummond, Fred, *All That Jazz*, p. 128
40 Imbach, Jeff, *The River Within*, p. 22

phrases such as 'Kissers Oink', 'Risen Kiosks' and 'Roe Skins Ski' all materialised from the rearranged letters of the leadership body that I happen to serve. However, can you imagine how pleased I was to notice that Kirk Session also comes out as RISKINESS OK? For a church body renowned for taking minutes and wasting hours, I had a wonderful new title to present to one and all.

"The risk-averse pursuit of safety is the quickest path to disaster" argues Professor Leonard Sweet, in his book *Soul Tsunami*. "Anyway: Since when did Jesus call his disciples to live a risk-free safety-first life? You want a conventional, convenient, consistent, predictable life? Then don't follow Jesus".[41] Sweet's friend, Brian McLaren, repeats a similar sentiment when he declares, "Jesus did not call us to a parking lot; he invited us on an adventure, an odyssey, a journey that will never end. Quite a difference".[42] Kirk Sessions take note!

Yet, it is not just Kirk Sessions that can be risk-averse. Every one of us need, at times, to be reminded that risk is, indeed, okay. Too often, the human condition is such that we'd rather stick with the familiar, keep ourselves comfortable and walk by the river's edge instead of getting out there on the turbulent waters ourselves.

In the spiritual realm, we are increasingly afraid also. We talk a good game and we may even pray boldly, but actually getting our sleeves rolled up and putting our faith into real action can be another matter altogether. Philip Yancey, author of the book *Prayer, Does it Make Any Difference*, reminds us that from God, "Streams of mercy flow". It's a pretty orthodox idea within the Christian tradition. Yancey follows up his statement, however, by asking a direct question about risk in regard to this aspect

41 Sweet, Leonard, *Soul Tsunami*, p. 98, 9
42 McLaren, Brian D., *More ready Than You Realise*, p. 140

of church life: "Will I stand by the bank or jump in the stream?"[43] Jump in the stream rather than stand on the bank? That's risky!

Now, it just happens that I heard Philip Yancey speaking about this book when, in 2008, I went on my annual trip to the brilliant Greenbelt Christian Arts Festival at Cheltenham race course, England. He mentioned this very concept about the stream of God's mercy and how we need to get right in there. The trouble was that I had been out on my kayak a day or two before, on the River Tay. Unfortunately, I had capsized and, as was pretty common at that stage in my new sporting passion, I hadn't managed to master my Eskimo roll in order to right my boat after it had overturned! You've got it; I swam! As a result, I listened to Yancey talking about us metaphorically getting into the water only a few hours after I had literally been in the largest waterway in Scotland where it had been cold and embarrassing and scary.

The river is deep and the current is strong and there are rocks that can do a lot of damage. That's the appeal! To quote Doug Ammons, "It's both a simple fact and a profound truth that the fun of kayaking comes in part from the potential danger of the river".[44]

Yet no wonder fear is a real feeling Christians experience when it comes to more than talking about living our life for Christ. Jumping into the stream really can be a risky business! As I've said, though, risk is okay whether spiritually or physically. After all, I'm a preacher and, as Harry Reid correctly reports in his book *Outside Verdict*, commissioned by a former Moderator of the Church of Scotland General Assembly, "To preach will require a cer-

---

43 Yancey, Philip, *Prayer – Does it Make Any Difference?*, p. 16
44 Ammons, Doug, *Whitewater Philosophy*, p. 33

tain amount of risk-taking and quite a lot of courage".[45]

There is another popular contemporary author whom I happen to have actually met at one of his book launches in Saddleback Church, Orange County, California. Strangely enough, it wasn't Revd Dr Rick Warren, pastor of the mega church at Saddleback who also prayed at President Obama's inauguration. No, the visiting speaker at Saddleback Church in July 2007 was John Ortberg, teaching pastor at Menlo Park Presbyterian Church, Santa Cruz. As I chatted to John he told me of his very fond memories of Scotland. He studied here, in the city of Aberdeen, under the Very Reverend Ian Pitt-Watson. As I read John's signed copy of his latest publication he told me, "A man can't just sit there. We must have challenge, risk, adventure. Only people who say yes to challenge, demand and risk, are ever fully alive".[46]

I completely agree! What is being said, really, is very similar to that phrase I mentioned before where Jesus said he came to give us "Life in all fullness" (John 10:10). In following Jesus Christ into his fullness of life, there can be inherent risks, which is exactly why I repeat that I'm sure our Lord would be delighted to have had a chance to go whitewater kayaking. As professor of Physical Education, Ron Watters says, "Risk makes our society healthier and more vibrant".[47] As the great physician, that's exactly what Jesus came to do.

Christ is the archetypal risk-taker. He reached out and touched lepers, something that in his time was a major no,

---

45 Reid, Harry, *Outside Verdict – An Old Kirk in a New Scotland*, p. 161

46 Ortberg, John, *When the Game is Over it All Goes Back in the Box*, p. 140

47 Quoted in Tao Berman, *Going Vertical – The Life of an Extreme Kayaker*, p. 117

no! He spoke to women when they were seen very much as being in the lower classes of society. He mixed with, and forgave, the most sinful of people so often that he was called a "glutton and a drunkard, a friend of tax collectors and sinners!" (Matthew 11:19). It wasn't a compliment! In fact, Jesus spoke out against the religious and political rulers of his day and challenged so much of the general thinking of the status quo, that he eventually was led to a cross for execution because of the hassle he had seemingly created. Here is a man who enjoyed and endured risky living indeed!

To quote Larry Christenson once more, "One day he [Jesus] rounded a sharp bend in the river. Dead ahead lay a treacherous stretch of rapids with a drop-off in clear sight – in the shape of a Roman cross. Jesus sensed that the Father's plan for his life went straight over the falls. Some of the party shouted in protest, 'Never, Lord. This shall never happen to you!' (Matthew 16:22). Jesus paddled out into midstream; he would ride this stretch of river alone".[48]

How preachers like me have dulled down this adventurous rebel with a cause I'll never know, for the last thing Jesus ever was, or ever shall be, is boring! In fact, if we still followed him with serious commitment today we would be taking all sorts of risks with the church's money, our congregation's talents and every one of our time schedules. But, generally, most of us prefer to sit in our pews or speak from our pulpits rather than get outside of the church into the real world to take some serious risky action. We prefer to play it safe.

It's fascinating, then, that in a terrific book on the history and content of the Bible, Karen Armstrong makes a very interesting point about our common humanity and

---

48 Christenson, Larry, *Ride the River*, p. 48

how each one of us actually need risk in order to feel more fully alive. She says, "Human beings seek *ekstasis*, a 'stepping out' of their normal, mundane experience. If they no longer find ecstasy in a synagogue, church or mosque, they look for it in dance, music, sport and drugs".[49]

Similarly, Maria Coffey, author and kayaker, says, "The inexorable yearning for something beyond the mundane or the explainable runs deep in the human psyche. It arises from an urge to find meaning in existence, for something bigger than ourselves".[50]

If both Armstrong and Coffey are correct, then maybe, just maybe, this aching for something more is one of the key reasons why, even though Christian activity holidays can be very much enjoyed and even inspirational, so many people of a younger generation have elected to vote with their feet, leaving churches on mass. It is just not dangerous, on edge, risky enough in our aptly named sanctuaries.

When I was reading a book called *Creating Uncommon Worship* by Revd Richard Giles about the renewal of church worship, I came across the following quote from someone I have mentioned elsewhere in my own writing here: Annie Dillard. She says, "It's madness to wear ladies' straw hats and velvet hats to church; we should all be wearing crash helmets. Ushers should issue life preservers and signal flares; they should lash us to our pews".[51] The Christian life, especially when worshipping the Creator of the universe, is a life full of risk and adventure.

This is a point of great importance, for the church has been at its strongest, most interesting and most world-changing when people like Revd Dr Martin Luther King Jr or Archbishop Desmond Tutu or Mother Teresa have

49 Armstrong, Karen, *The Bible – The Biography*, p. 5
50 Coffey, Maria, *Explorers of the Infinite*, p. 7
51 Quoted in Giles, Richard, *Creating Uncommon Worship*, p. 9

been at the helm. Whether entering into the treacherous waters of racial abuse, segregation or extreme poverty, where others have tragically perished along the way, the majority of humanity has generally rallied behind such inspirational risk-takers and has backed such church life to the hilt. Christianity can be an extreme faith just as kayaking can be an extreme sport. In fact, risk-taking ought to be the norm!

Certainly, every book I have read on the subject of kayaking agrees that risk-taking is the norm for the sport. Just listen to a few of the experts here:

"Running whitewater in a small boat is inherently dangerous. In fact, the danger is part of the appeal."[52]

Wayne Dickert who competed in the 1996 Olympics.

"Any activity that takes place around water has the potential to lead to tricky situations that can quickly become serious dangers."[53]

2006 downriver racing world champion kayaker, Jodi Bigelow

"Whitewater kayaking is a technical sport with specialised equipment and some inherent risks".[54]

Ken Whiting, recognised by *Paddler Magazine* as one of their Paddlers of the Century.

In the guidebook to the whitewater of my home country of Scotland, indeed, there is a health warning right at the start: "Paddlers should need no reminding that whitewater

---

52 Dickert, Wayne, *Basic Kayaking*, p. 81
53 Bigelow, Jodi, *Kayaking for Fitness*, p. 62
54 Whiting, Ken, *Whitewater Kayaking – The Ultimate Guide*, p. xiv

paddling is an adventure sport involving an element of uncertainty and risk taking".[55]

With so many warnings and stories of danger and risk, is it any wonder that so many good, church-going, God-following Christians are nowhere to be seen on the river? It's much safer, and allegedly more sensible, to stay inside centrally heated or air-conditioned church buildings to sing some hymns and say some prayers and listen to yet another sermon. As referred to in Jeff Imbach's book *The River Within*, "We warn people about the dangers of life but never invite them to go out and face the dangers bravely".[56]

On one of my first ever trips on a river, upon learning what I did for a living, a rather astute fellow kayaker asked me what the members of my church felt about their minister taking part in such a risky sport. "Oh, be careful, Scott, that's very dangerous", is exactly what I told my new friend. Indeed, that is the very thing that several people had said. And sure enough, in the church, time and again, I've been told I'm "off my head", "a nutter" or "crazy". People are seeing the risk in my hobby but are not as aware of the necessity for risk in my vocation.

To be honest, I appreciate the concern and fully understand the sentiments (which I'll develop a little more in the next chapter). But I am also alarmed to a degree that, in the church, we have a tendency to steer well clear of anything and everything that is risky. In my reading of Matthew, Mark, Luke or John, it is quite clear that the whole idea of following Jesus was never going to make for a life of ease and comfort!

"Take up your cross and follow me" (Mark 8:34) is one central phrase of interest. A cross for Jesus was no

55 Thomas, Bridget (Ed), *Scottish Whitewater*, p. 7
56 Imbach, Jeff, *The River Within*, p. 39

nicely carved piece of church ornamentation, nor was it a beautifully polished piece of jewellery. The cross was an instrument of the most horrific torture and execution invented by that most brutal of regimes who ruled the Roman Empire. Christians are instructed to pick up a cross and follow? That sounds a bit risky to me, as well as being something to be expected if we are to take seriously Thomas à Kempis, in his *Imitation of Christ* from the 15th century: "The whole life of Christ was a cross and martyrdom; and do you look for rest and selfish pleasure? You are greatly mistaken if you look for anything save to endure trials, for all this mortal life is full of troubles and everywhere marked with crosses".[57]

In the absolutely superb passage known as the Beatitudes in Matthew's Gospel, Jesus also tells it straight: "People will insult you and hurt you and say all sorts of evil things against you because you follow me" (Matthew 5:11). Again, if that doesn't sound like we need to employ a good dose of risk management in our Christian discipleship, then I am not entirely sure what does.

Perhaps the even greater risk assessment needs to be made in regard to one of Jesus' greatest and most difficult commands of all: to "Love your enemies". Such teaching is laden with jeopardy. We could be laughed at, walked over, taken for a fool – or beaten so badly that it actually kills us. Seriously. In one of his magnificent sermons on such matters of non-violence, the heroic Christ-follower, Revd Dr Martin Luther King Jr was clear: "To our most bitter opponents we say: We shall match your capacity to inflict suffering with our capacity to endure suffering. We shall meet your physical force with soul force. Do to us what you will, and we shall continue to love you . . . throw us in

---

57 Thomas à Kempis, *The Imitation of Christ*, p. 86

jail and we shall still love you. Send your hooded perpetrators of violence into our community at the midnight hour and beat us and leave us half dead, and we shall still love you. But be assured that we will wear you down with our capacity to suffer. One day we shall win freedom. . ."[58]

Because of the challenge and power of such messages of indescribable risk-taking, on a trip to exchange pulpits in 2005 with Revd Holton Siegling of First Presbyterian Church, Marion South Carolina, I sat in Ebenezer Baptist Church on Auburn Avenue, Atlanta, Georgia with tears running down my cheeks. I'd flown into Atlanta and stopped off for a visit to where MLK had been pastor. During that visit I longed that I might be a man of God who would risk my life for the sake of that which is right and true and good. Christianity is most definitely not risk-free and we fool ourselves grievously if we allow the safety and comfort of the pew to let us think otherwise.

To turn to the kayaking once more, as I write this particular passage, I do appreciate that kayaking in whitewater is a very, very real risk. I am still in the same shock that the rest of the kayaking world is facing in the tragic death of Chris Wheeler. Disastrously, Chris, a very experienced kayaking instructor and regular contributor to Canoe & Kayak magazine, drowned on the swollen river Dart on Sunday 21st November 2009 in the immense spate conditions after heavy rainfalls.

For Chris's family and friends, the devastating news of the loss of a great man, in terrible circumstances, must be unbearable. I simply cannot imagine! Nor can the mental trauma and anguish be fathomed of those friends on the river, who desperately fought to save Chris who was trapped by a tangle of trees and undergrowth. And

---

58 King, Martin Luther, *Strength to Love*, p. 54

yet, someone with Chris's 25 year's worth of international kayaking knowledge and experience would be fully aware of the many dangers involved. He dislocated his knees when he went over the Conwy falls in the 1980s after all! The extremely high levels were the attraction to the Dart that terrible day and I know that the inherent risk would never have been taken lightly. It all went terribly wrong because of a combination of tragic circumstances, but risk was *always* there on *every* trip. Chris would have agreed, I'm sure, with the following quote.

"Security is mostly a superstition", says Helen Keller, "It does not exist in nature, nor do the children of men as a whole experience it. Avoiding danger in the long run is no safer than outright exposure. Life is either a daring adventure or nothing".[59]

Risk, despite the real dangers of death, helps us live. That's what whitewater kayaking does for me – it provides an opportunity to get out of the office or the pulpit to do something different and risky and challenging. I love it for the beauty of God's creation, the exercise I get, the people I meet and the new skills and spiritual lessons it teaches me.

In truth, leaving the office or pulpit and walking around the corner to the high street shops, may not actually be any less risky, but you'll know that if you've ever heard of Bobby Leach. In 1911 Leach was the first man to ever go over the Niagara Falls in a barrel. He survived, as mad as the whole event was! Alas, he did die only 15 years later when he slipped on a piece of orange peel on a pavement in Christchurch, New Zealand!

Yes kayaking can be risky (and I do not make that comment flippantly). But, it would appear that doing the

---

59 Quoted in *Failing Forward* by John C. Maxwell, p. 127

most mundane of things can be risky too. If Jesus said, "I have come that you might have life in all fullness" I'm going to take him at his word, making sensible risk-assessments along the way. Are you up for some fullness of life?

Be Strong and Courageous

"*The human journey is not easy. Nor is it simple.*"

Matthew Fox, *One River, Many Wells*, p. 2

"*Life is difficult.*"

Scott M. Peck, *The Road Less Travelled*, p. 15

OK – warning! If you think I've quoted a lot (maybe even too much) from Doug Ammons already (which I highlighted at the start I would do) you're really going to love me now! In this chapter I think I quote him three times in sizeable mouthfuls. The reason for this, however, is not something to apologise for because in his book *Whitewater Philosophy* Doug has written extensively and expansively on the very subject I address here. If my writing whets your appetite for the issue that this chapter raises, I heartily advise you to get a copy of Ammons' book! It's well worth it. In fact, contact him directly and he'll maybe even scribe a wee personal message on it like he did to mine! For now, you'll just have to settle for my 'pearls of wisdom'.

On a beginners kayak course a couple of years back I remember the instructor, Doug Cooper, encouraging all the participants by saying that we will all make great whitewater-warriors one day. I had to laugh. I'm more a whitewater-worrier than a whitewater-warrior myself! I have, since then, paddled on Scotland's largest river, the Tay, many times over. On several occasions I have even kayaked successfully through the more exciting rapids of the Grandtully section where there is, in the middle of the rapid, a rock, which, for very good reason, is called "boat-breaker".[60]

I also happen to have had wonderful times paddling down the upper and lower sections of the River Tummel which is one of the rivers on which BBC presenter Gryff Rhys Jones paddled a canoe for a documentary on the waterways of Great Britain. He said of it, "Clearly we were off on an adventure . . . we went at a terrifying rate, alone except for the camera boat on a river that was surging downstream. . . . We were going at an unacceptable rate without paddling at all. . . . I was scared. . . . I was right to be scared".[61] With its gnarly holes that can trap you and the double drop waterfall called the Linn, which flows powerfully into Loch Faskally, there is no question that the river Tummel in rural Perthshire holds some extreme excitement for the paddler brave enough to tackle it.

On one particular day, however, I was no longer in the familiarity of Perthshire with my big hunk of beautiful blue polyethylene called a Dagger GT. This day, my faithful Vauxhall Vectra car clocked up a few more miles to take it closer to the 100 000 mile mark as we headed along the A82 into the highland glen where the river Etive flows. It was promising to be a fine day out. We were just around

---

60 Tragically, in April 2010, nineteen year old Simon Fletcher died in this very spot due to "a one-in-a-million accident" during spate conditions on the swollen river. *Herald Newspaper*, April 8th 2010

61 Jones, Gryff Rhys, *Rivers*, pp. 32–35

the corner from the sensational scenery of Glencoe with all its high mountain crags, the wild deer that roam them, and the bloody history of clan at war with clan. The snag was that I was having a small personal battle of my own as we considered kayaking down a river that is described thus:

"Triple falls is a good test of nerve. . . . Beware the undercut boulder on the right. . ." then "the first real test of your journey. Crack of Doom (Gd 4+). . . "[62]

"Crack of Doom"! They name sections of rivers this way in order to put the fear of death into little wimpy inter-mediate kayakers like me, just in case we weren't already thinking about what hymns to have sung at our funeral already. I sang a verse of *Abide with Me* right there on the spot!

I can feel my heart palpitations beginning all over again as I even just sit here in the safety of my study, sitting as I am describing events on my laptop. On that particular day in Glen Etive, you'll appreciate, I was terrified. Well, when I say 'terrified', I wasn't frightened enough to actually strip out of my wetsuit, re-strap my kayak back onto the car roof, and head back to the pub for a nice gentle game of dominoes you understand. Nevertheless, to say that I was just feeling apprehensive would be to make a rather large understatement.

I made it through all the 'interesting' drops that the river had to offer with only one swim at 'Letterbox' and one portage at 'Crack of Dawn'. But then we came upon 'Big Man Falls' and I was required to make a decision – wimp out and turn my kayaking hobby into a spectator sport, or join in with my pal, Ross, and the other six wonderful new kayaking friends I had met from Switzerland.

---

62 Jackson, Andy, *Scottish Whitewater*, p. 184

Here was the idea: to plunge over the edge of a six metre drop which must have had tonne after tonne of water flooding into the pool below.

Here was the hope: that I would manage to drop into that torrent without rearranging my facial features with my paddle shaft smashing into them as my whole body collided with the watery depths below. I then had to manage an Eskimo roll back up again, after rising to the surface (with luck!).

Here was the problem: I was being overwhelmed by a four-letter word, beginning with the letter 'f'.

Fear – it's the same old thing that the angels told Mary and Joseph not to have when they suddenly appeared before them prior to the very first Christmas. Fear – it's the stuff that Jesus scolded his disciples for having when a storm suddenly rose up on Lake Galilee when he and they had been out on a boat. Fear – it's an ordinary, natural, sensation that holy (and unholy) people have been known to encounter, and I have had my fair share along the way. I'm grateful, then, to read Lito Tejada-Flores in *Wildwater* stating, "Fear is a nebulous yet terribly important aspect of whitewater boating".[63] And I'm grateful, of course, to the ever philosophical Doug Ammons: "Fear is something that many kayakers have to face at some point, but yet it is also something that many experienced kayakers don't talk about at all, leaving newcomers to work their way through what can easily become a psychological minefield. . . . Fear is a totally normal and good thing". [64]

Despite this 'f' word, the situation described above on the River Etive is the interesting type of situation that whitewater kayakers put themselves into all the time, and it all needs a bit of courage.

63 Tejada-Flores, Lito, *Wildwater*, p. 154
64 Ammons, Doug, *Whitewater Philosophy*, pp. 124, 125

So, what did I do? With a permanent marker pen, I signed the laminated copy of my will which I hastily drew up on my Blackberry, I made a last phone call home to tell my wife and children that I love them very much, and I genuflected even though I'm not a Roman Catholic. Then I paddled over that, to me, horrific drop which lasted several seconds less than the time it took me to resurface (upside down) from the murky depths below. As Robert O. Collins and Roderick Nash say in their book, *The Big Drops: Ten Legendary Rapids,* "Defining a big drop is almost as difficult as running one. One man's terror is another man's piece of cake".[65] Well, for this particular man this big drop, was *my* absolute terror. After it, the plunge was my piece of cake. I did manage to Eskimo roll back upright again, you see, and wow, did it feel fantastic!

I've been here before in similar circumstances as a Christian. Not only do I do something every week, called public speaking, (which I am told is one of the biggest fears most people have) but I can recall the time I was asked to speak at a youth club in a rougher part of Glasgow than I was used to during the initial stages of my faith. I sat in the gent's toilets of the church hall and I prayed for strength and opened the Bible at random since I was clutching it in my white-knuckled hands anyway.

"Be strong and courageous",[66] the words read, as God told Joshua to get a grip of himself now that he was taking the helm after Moses had died. Presumably Joshua was having a "Big Man Falls" moment, just a little anxious about what lay up ahead. No shame on him! Moses also had been less than bold when the mantle of leadership was placed upon his shoulders prior to Joshua.

---

65 Quoted in Tao Berman, *Going Vertical – The Life of an Extreme Kayaker*, p. 137

66 Joshua 1:9

The Bible tells us in Exodus chapter three that when Moses saw the burning bush he was "afraid". A few paragraphs later, when God speaks to him, this big hero of Israel cries out in a stuttering voice, "Who am I, that I should go to Pharaoh and bring the Israelites out of Egypt?" After some words of reassurance from the Almighty, he again protests, "Suppose I go to the Israelites and say to them, 'The God of your fathers has sent me to you,' and they ask me, 'What is his name?' Then what shall I tell them?"

Throughout the encounter, you get the distinct feeling that Moses isn't keen. He is nervous. He is apprehensive. He is downright scared. So God gives an answer that should remain with each one of us in every situation that causes our face to whiten, our knees to knock and our teeth to clench: "I am who I am. This is what you are to say to the Israelites: 'I AM' has sent me to you.'"

Note that the response is not, "I have been who I have been" or "I will be who I will be". The promise is, "I AM" – God with us in the present tense. From Gideon, to Jonah, to King David, to all the characters of the New Testament too, finding inner confidence to follow where God leads has been the order of the day, if you read about the Bible characters who followed their faith instincts.

Should we be any more surprised, then, if *we* set out to do interesting things in the church, or on a river? No. There are bound to always be situations that demand things of us that we're not sure we can give, but, "He does not leave us alone in our struggles" asserts the Revd Dr Martin Luther King Jr.[67] That's what it means to have faith. That said, I do wonder why, if God was with me that night in the youth group, why he didn't stop some of the teenagers setting my hair on fire!! The prank by those less than innocent

---

67 King, Martin Luther, Jr, *Strength to Love*, p. 16

youth group members was only noticed when some of my fellow leaders spotted flames licking up the back of my skull! I suppose it was God's way of saying, 'get a haircut'. (It was rather long at the time, I recall!)

Another time that I can recall finding myself lacking in confidence was on one less than ordinary November day in 2004 as I arose from my slumber in my first ministry in Fife. As the radio alarm woke me up, it did so announcing sound-bites of the local, national and international news. Unfortunately, on this particular day, the local, national and international news all arrived in one package. Pte Paul Lowe, a 19-year-old infantryman from the Black Watch Battalion of the British Army had been killed by a suicide bomber in Basra, Iraq. Along with two other servicemen who were killed in the incident, Paul was from West Fife. Indeed, Paul was from the village where I was minister.

I'll never know the courage of the service personnel who seek to protect the freedom of our democratic country by standing on the front lines and defending us from brutality and carnage, buffeting us as they do with their very own bodies. But this day I did feel the fear of not knowing the first thing to say to Paul's mum, Helen, or other members of the Lowe family, including Brother Craig who was also serving in Iraq. I'm quite sure I never found any words of comfort that were in any way truly meaningful, but I do know now that it is a brave thing to go and simply be there beside someone in these thin places between life and death.

I prayed and I dug deep down inside myself to find all the courage I could summon, and I jumped right into the powerful, fast-flowing, turbulent rapids of tears and heartache which such a section of life's river brings. What I found upon entry to the troubled waters was that others had already plunged in before me, such is the humbling beauty and innate goodness of humanity. Together, family, friends and a nervous minister, tried to navigate each other through to calmer stretches of water as best we possibly could.

Confidence and courage do not simply appear within us out of nowhere. Fear can be a very powerful and paralysing emotion and, in many ways, as if our inner self-protection system is not enough, we are culturally raised to be cautious. 'Be careful how you carry those scissors', 'Don't swing so high on that rope', 'Stay away from the edge of that pond' we are told over and over again throughout childhood. I can still hear my late father telling me to keep away from the edge of St. Rule's tower at St. Andrews ruined Abbey some 35 years ago. His plea for caution came despite the fact that I was all of 3 ft tall and the wall in front of me was higher! Out of concern for our loved ones' safety, we seek to breed a sensible respect for danger. Might such caution not also wrap us in a little much cotton wool too?

What's Doug Ammons' opinion? Well, thanks for asking! "If we boil down all the questions we have about whitewater and kayaking, past all the questions about fun and beauty, about excitement and challenge, right down to the single thing that was most critical, that question might be, 'will I die if I mess up and have to swim that rapid?' Death is the very last thing any of us have on our minds as we head out to paddle. The problem is, there is never any guarantee of what might happen."[68]

There never has been any guarantee of what might happen and there never will be! Certainly, we tend to forget that the world of the Bible was one where natural dangers would be all around: wild animals on the prowl, bacteria

68 Ammons, Doug, *Whitewater Philosophy*, p. 109

lurking in unhygienic or non-existent sanitation, no health and safety officer at the local synagogue! When someone said, "Trust in God", they really, really meant 'trust in God'. Even for us now, despite all the medical developments, healthier diets and safety gear that we can amass, there are still occasions when all we have is a prayer. Life still is a fragile thing, and it always will be, so the paradoxical mixture of confidence and caution will be requirements for us all forever.

It is a faith thing, whether seeking to be a good shepherd of your flock on a Galilean hillside, hesitantly waiting your turn to ferry glide across some turbulent river, or thinking about responding to a call to get more involved in God's work in the world. Again, John Ortberg gets it right. "The choice to follow Jesus – the choice to grow – is the choice for the constant recurrence of fear... this means that to be a follower of Jesus you must renounce comfort as the ultimate value of your life."[69] Faith can help us to be less anxious about being anxious; faith in God, faith in our assessment of the dangers, faith in the safety strategies we should put in place if needed.

As the Danish philosopher, Soren Kierkegaard, once said, "The person who has learnt to be afraid in the right way has learnt the most important lesson of all".[70]

As the American philosopher, Doug Ammons, also says, "How do you deal with this? The best way is proactively, do everything you can to prepare yourself solidly so you are less likely to be thrown out of control and feel threatened to begin with. Greater competence, control, skill and

69 Ortberg, John, *If You Want to Walk on Water You've Got to Get Out of the Boat*, p 21

70 The Concept of Dread (quoted in Moltmann Experiences of God, p. 39)

understanding are the best way to deal with fear – because they allow you to avoid it in the first place".[71]

Breaking things down to work out exactly what we are scared of definitely can help. When someone is fearful of sharing his faith with another, for instance, is the anxiety about not knowing enough about the professed faith or is it in being laughed at or rejected by friends who you happen to choose to talk with? Both issues could freeze us from ever engaging with personal evangelism, but they both need to be handled differently. Not knowing enough can be countered by reading, studying or learning more about that which we are unclear, so as to raise confidence and develop a better base of knowledge. The worry about being laughed at or rejected is far more about self esteem and security in relationships and needs to be handled by assessing how much we trust those with whom we are conversing. Most likely, if we speak with respect of other peoples' views, those very same people will retort with respect for ours. Often such an anxiety is greatly over-emphasised and the fear is actually unfounded.

In kayaking we also do well to try and articulate exactly what it is we are frightened of if we are showing severe apprehension about one thing or another. We can be worried about looking like a fool when we don't manage an Eskimo roll attempt or we can be anxious that those who will need to rescue us in such an event will find us to be an irritant. Alternatively, we might be frightened that, when we capsize, we will be trapped in the boat, unable to breathe again and, ultimately, drown. Each possibility is quite different from the other, yet the feeling of apprehension may be the same. Take some time then to assess what it is, specifically, that is making you less than confident in

---

71 Ammons, Doug, *Whitewater Philosophy*, p. 151

one way or another. Then understand your feelings a little better, and take the specific steps necessary to create ways of conquering, or at least handling, that which would hold you back.

Fear begins in the mind as we tell ourselves that we can't do this or we can't do that. But authors of *Manage Your Mind*, Gillian Butler and Tony Hope, helpfully advise, "It is best to face difficulties instead of avoiding them; to acknowledge the difficulty instead of denying it is there".[72] Very interestingly from the point of view of our subject matter, the authors continue, "Each time you avoid something you fear, it becomes more likely that you will avoid it again at the next opportunity, like a river which cuts deeper and deeper into its bed".[73]

Our fear can wear us down! We are best to try not to let it get the better of us. Focus upon exactly what it is, then, that is causing exceptional caution in your life, and be bold and be strong and do what you never thought possible. Have faith in yourself! Courage is not the absence of fear, but having fear and doing that something anyway. "The brave admit their fears", says Dominican Friar, Timothy Radcliffe, and "The first stage in becoming brave is liberation from unreal fears, from being afraid of things that are not really dangerous".[74] Further, as another one of my ministerial colleagues says in his book, *Creating Healthy Churches*, "Knowing what we are afraid of gives us some sense of control".[75]

Ultimately I suppose, in kayaking, people are most worried about dying! The terrible tragedy I've mentioned in

72 Butler, Gillian & Hope, Tony, *Manage Your Mind*, p. 47

73 Butler, Gillian & Hope, Tony, *Manage Your Mind*, p. 196

74 Radcliffe, Timothy, O.P., *What is the Point of Being a Christian*, pp. 72, 73

75 Richardson, Ronald W., *Creating a Healthier Church*, p. 43

footnotes in this very chapter, and the quotes that I shared earlier about risks in kayaking, all reveal that there are inherent dangers. The worst case scenario of all is that there would be a fatality on the river. Well here, as a minister, I am very well qualified to write – not because I have died already and come back to spout forth my wisdom, but because in my thirteen-year career as a pastor in a local church I have conducted over six hundred funerals. In fact, death is one subject that convinces me more than any other of the reality of a spiritual realm, even if it is the last taboo.

People don't like to talk of death I have learnt. Speak, instead, of someone 'passing away', or 'going to be with granddad', or 'being a star in heaven'. We are scared of this aspect of our lives in a way that our ancestors would never have struggled with such finality. This can cause us real problems, for our fears about death can tend to obscure our thinking about life. As theologian Jurgen Moltmann has said, "Anxiety blurs vision and judgement".[76]

21st century western humanity is afraid, I think, because, like any river we just don't have all the answers to who we are, where we have come from and where we are going. That is one of the reasons why we need to find our course along the way to the final unknown as best as we can. Our journey remains as much of a mystery to us as it did to our forefathers, irrespective of however many scientific answers we have to how many things work.

The first time I encountered a dead body was when a member of our Kelty Kirk choir died. One Sunday morning Robert had been praising his Maker, but before the next weekend came around he had *met* his Maker. I went to the funeral home to pay my respects because I was as

---

76 Moltmann, Jurgen, *Experiences of God*, p. 38

shocked by the sudden passing of this gentleman as anyone else, except, I'm sure, his lovely wife Nan. There Robert lay in his coffin, so dignified, so still, so cold. But I did not recognise him as the man I knew. The Mr Muir that I had known was a happy man, a bright man, a positive man. Yet here lay his body without any life in it. All the spirit he had possessed was gone. Gone where though? Just disappeared into the ether or 'gone to a better place' as we clergy like to say?

I've experienced so many people in bereavement that a different question has arisen for me now; not so much where has the spirit of that person gone to, but how did that spirit get into the person in the first place? What constitutes 'life', and where does it come from? As the materialistic atheist would demand that we believe, are human beings really only muscle and blood cells and bone and fat; matter which in the end doesn't really matter? Or is the person sitting in an eddy at the top of a waterfall more than all these things combined: a man or woman of spirituality as well as a man or woman of physicality? Are we soul as well as skeleton and sinew and skin?

Many seldom think on such matters because so many of us operate from a modern, scientific point of view. Life has, for many, been reduced to biology and DNA and physiology. That's not life though, that's discourse about the physical matter that has life within. Life itself is something altogether more intangible, mysterious indeed. And the life in all fullness that I have mentioned a few times now is something far beyond scientific discussion.

I love, in this regard, Dr Francis Collins' book, *The Language of God*. Collins, at the time of writing, was the head of the Human Genome Project, a world leader in life's code. It is remarkable to me that such a scientific-ally advanced mind can still state in 2007 the following:

"DNA, with its phosphate-sugar backbone and intricately arranged organic bases, stacked neatly on top of one another and paired together at each rung of the twisted double helix, seems an utterly improbable molecule to have 'just happened' – especially since DNA seems to possess no intrinsic means of copying itself. . . . There are good reasons to believe in God".[77]

I've thought for a long time that there are good reasons to believe in God, even if I have not always had a very good appreciation or understanding of all things scientific.

Actually, I think that's why I'm attracted to the river in the first place. The river is bigger than me; so is God. The river's been there longer than me; God is eternal. The river will be there even when I've taken my last breath; God is called Alpha and Omega, beginning and end. And on those rivers I see something of my vulnerable self; the same little self I see in the presence of God when I pray. On the river I am reminded that I am really very small, that my life is fragile and that I do well to remember such facts. Religion has been reminding humanity of such things for thousands of years. And so I praise God for the life I have within me – my spirit, my soul, my inner being. I thank him for the beauty of the places I paddle, the adventure of the trips I find myself on, and the challenges to be less afraid.

Actually, I'm not sure that I do fear things less when the water is buffeting me or the rocks are getting a little close or my roll just isn't as bomb-proof as I'd like. I am, though, more able to sense that I'm not on my own and that there is a higher purpose. I do try and learn to do what the Angels and Jesus instruct: "Fear not". I'm not going to pretend to have managed it completely overnight or even mastering it at all. I am certain, however, that I'm going to

---

77 Collins, Francis, *The Language of God*, pp. 91, 93

do my utmost to die living to the full. That will simply take a little courage, but, as the great adventurer Bear Grylls says, "Nature isn't something to be feared, but relished".[78] I'm trying.

---

78 Grylls, Bear, *Born Survivor*, p. 9

Capsizing

"Never give up, for even rivers someday wash dams away"

Arthur Golden[79]

By now you will have heard me mention capsizing a few times, not least because I've done it quite often! Mainly I've mentioned this tendency to look at the fish through very watery eyes when talking about my passion of kayaking. Time and time again, though, I have been known to capsize pretty efficiently in daily life too! Caught out often by my own inefficient actions, or some circumstance beyond my control, I have failed to stay upright in the way I seek to live as a Christian, as a father, as a husband and as a man.

The bottom line is that, in many of the things that tempt me, I sometimes lose my balance. One minute I'm paddling along quite nicely on some warm easy current, the next I find my head deep under the water, without a hope of a breath. No matter how much I try and no matter how long I've been on the good ship Christianity, I just can't seem to master each skill that would prevent me tipping too far one way or another.

---

79 Arthur Golden, http://www.brainyquote.com/qoutes/authors/a/arthur_golden.html

You could call me a hypocrite, actually. I say I believe certain things and I don't always live up to such high standards consistently. But, then, I have a sneaky suspicion that I could call you one too. Is it your chocolate addiction or your promise to spend more time with the kids or your language that you'd never use in front of your Grandmother? "Every one of us falls from grace" says author, Leonard Sweet. "Not one of us can claim total consistency between who we are and who we claim we are. No one gets through life without being capsized by a thousand compromises."[80]

Christian, Muslim, Atheist or Agnostic, we all have habits and traits that push us further to one side than we'd like, so capsizing in life is something we all are going to have to handle. When it comes to people of faith, for sure, church walls are only full of sinners *learning* to be saints. This minister is no different and it's definitely in this area of kayaking that I've learnt some of my biggest spiritual lessons!

Someone who professes to follow Jesus Christ is simply saying that they want to learn from this master holy man about how they too might be more righteous in their living. I know that is why I am a Christian anyway. A good little story makes the point well.

One day, after a stormy night, a minister was out in the manse garden attempting to fix a piece of fencing that had been blown down by the prevailing wind of the evening before. With hammer in hand the minister noticed a child from the neighbourhood watching his every move. "I hope you're not looking to pick up any tips in joinery", says the minister to his young parishioner. "Oh no", laughs the lad, "I'm just waiting here to see what a minister says when he hits his thumb with a hammer."

---

80 Leonard Sweet, *Summoned to Lead*, p. 36

Nice one. What do you think a minister says in such a situation? "Oh, thank you Lord for this time of trial and all that I can learn from the experience." Eh, nope. Ministers and church members are ordinary human beings, and, as such, we are prone to capsizing in life over and over and over again. It's normal, it's natural and really ought to be expected.

As I've mentioned before, the Super Scrappy kayak helmet I own is covered in some pretty interesting scrapes, coming, as they do, from my frequent encounters with submerged rocks. I've been tempted to use a marker pen to write the details of each incident beside each scuff. The trouble is that there wouldn't be enough surface area to record all the facts. That is even more the case in regard to the number of marks there would be were all my misdeeds being recorded somewhere. Maybe they are!

Since this chapter is not about my personal public confession, however, I won't lead *you* into the temptation of gossiping behind my back by providing all my struggles with the seven deadly sins. My publisher has, after all, given me a set word count to work to! It is sufficient to acknowledge, shall we say, that I am a less-than-perfect-Christian who is something of a capsizing expert. I am, also, it would appear, in rather good, biblical company.

- Adam (with forbidden fruit) capsized.
- Samson (with Delilah) capsized.
- Noah (with wine) capsized.
- King David (with Bathsheba) capsized.

"God uses people who fail – cause there ain't any other kind around", states John C. Maxwell in his book, *Failing Forwards*.[81] Amen to that!

---

81 Maxwell, John C., *Failing Forwards*, p. 27

True, there are some outside the church who like to point the finger at we 'hypocrites', but they tend to forget that when they do so there are three fingers pointing straight back at them. There are also some inside the church who like to think that they are holier than others, but they have forgotten that the Bible warns against such sanctimonious attitudes. "*All* have sinned and fallen short of the glory of God"[82] (italics mine). "If you think you're standing firm be careful that you don't fall."[83]

Splash! It doesn't take much for the most experienced of paddlers to find themselves wetting their hair. Splash! It doesn't take much for the most experienced Christian to be flipped. Splash! Such is this real, twisting, undulating, river of life. It's going to catch us all out once or twice or many times over. We'd better prepare to roll back up, which is what conversion is all about.

In his book, *A Call to Conversion*, Jim Wallis verifies this when he writes, "In the Bible, conversion means, 'turning'. . ." and "Conversion begins with repentance, the Greek word for which is *metanoia*".[84] In my Greek dictionary that I use loads because the New Testament was mainly written in that language, the word *metanoia* is defined as "a change as would reverse the effects of [his] own previous state".[85] It seems to me that this is the same definition as an Eskimo roll! That means turning too!

Mastering an Eskimo roll is one of the best skills you can acquire as a kayaker. It's what's going to give you your best chance at righting yourself every time the inevitable happens. Likewise, it is sensible to learn how to get right

---

82 Romans 3:23
83 1 Corinthians 10:12
84 Wallis, Jim, *A Call to Conversion*, p. 3
85 Vine, W.E., *Expository Dictionary of New Testament Words*, p. 281

side up again when circumstances have knocked us over the edge in our day to day lives.

Actually, there are various kinds of 'Eskimo' rolls: the C to C roll, the sweep roll, the back deck roll. Each one requires slightly different technique and a whole lot of practice and patience. Yet, for whatever method employed, the first thing to do is to acknowledge that we *have* actually capsized. Not surprisingly, this part isn't so difficult. The water flooding up your nostrils and your lungs struggling to function normally give the biggest clues!

Once acknowledged, there is a set pattern to follow and physical motions to go through: set up, catch and recovery. Set up is where we position our body under the water so as we might have the best chance of turning the boat right side up again. The catch phase is where we use our paddle blade to grab as much water to support our upper body as we use our lower body to rotate around. In the recovery phase we, counter intuitively, keep our head as low to the water as possible and make sure it is the last thing up.

In the world of spiritual capsize, rolling is not so different. It is, as I said, known as repentance; turning ourselves round 180 degrees and choosing to follow the path we ought to have followed in the first place. In his book, *Prayer*, Richard Foster correctly says that we need this form of righting ourselves, "not just once, but again and again".[86]

Interestingly, the acknowledgement of the need of repentance will not be as easy as our acknowledgement of our need of an Eskimo roll. "Repentance is like exercise or dieting in some ways" says Brian McLaren in *Finding Faith*, "Just about everyone needs it, but it is amazingly easy to avoid".[87] As human beings, we have developed an

---

86 Foster, Richard, *Prayer*, p. 43
87 McLaren, Brian D., *Finding Faith*, p. 191

amazing capacity at fooling ourselves into believing that we haven't really capsized when we have. None of us like to dwell on the fact that we've mucked things up if we can possibly manage to avoid it! As Mark Twain once quipped, "Denial ain't just a river in Egypt".[88] But denial won't right our boat.

Once we do admit that, actually, we might be to blame for some of the messy stuff of life, set up will be about our learning to comfortably adopt a position of meekness for sincere, prayerful confession. Words like 'sorry,' 'confess,' or 'mercy' will all then act like the blade of a paddle, helping us catch the living water of God's ever-flowing grace. As we then enter the recovery phase, it is not unhelpful to keep our heads bowed low in healthy humility, until the very end of our prayer of confession. Obviously, when we have capsized in life, it is quite natural to feel a sense of shame, but once righted, once dealt with, it is not helpful to keep on staying low. We are forgiven, we are absolved of our wrong so, as in kayaking, it is good to adopt a nice positive posture and journey onward with good intent, at least until the next splash!

My old friend, Coach John Wooden, says, "Failure is a necessary ingredient of success".[89] Too true! Whether in learning to ride the river or in learning to walk in faith, we *are* going to capsize. I know I have done so, dramatically, in both areas. The big mistake is in not learning from the mistakes we make or in thinking that, because we've failed, we are, by definition, a failure. It's not so. Someone who keeps on capsizing and works hard at rolling back up is no failure. He is a dedicated learner who will one day, over time, develop a bomb-proof roll. A person who

88 http://en.thinkexist.com/quotation/denial_ain-t_just_a_river_in_egypt/214895.html

89 Wooden, John and Jamison, Steve, *Wooden on Leadership*, p. 37

continually stumbles on the straight and narrow path of life, and works hard at always getting back up after a fall, is what the Bible simply calls a disciple.

Have you ever noticed how closely connected that word 'disciple' is to the very similar word, 'discipline'? There's a reason. Being perfect as Christ was perfect is going to take some discipline – and most of us (eh, make that all of us!) are going to struggle to get close! But it's okay. There's no need to beat ourselves up all the time. As long as we know we are trying our best, God will know that too! We just need to keep on keeping on.

Little by little, bit by bit we can become what we need to become, but not by remaining what we are. "Mistakes are inevitable when you are a novice", say the authors of *Manage Your Mind*. "In fact, they are an important part of the learning process."[90]

I learnt this lesson, once more, in July 2009. During this time, I had the terrific opportunity to exchange pulpits in Fernandina Beach, Florida, on the beautiful Amelia Island at the very north of the Sunshine State. There is no white-water in Florida, so the only paddling I would be able to do was in the alligator infested, flat-water creeks and in the shark infested sea. I didn't have any gear with me but I had met a great guy on the social networking website Facebook who said he was prepared to share his equipment with me. Steve Bott, who kayak surfs Fernandina Beach's waves regularly, was more than happy for me to try out this new aspect of the sport (for me) using his boat and paddles. I was so grateful.

Steve gave me a quick lesson and a quick demonstration of how to paddle out over the breakers, how to catch a wave and how to use your paddle as a rudder to guide

---

90 Butler, Gillian and Hope, Tony, *Manage Your Mind*, p. 92

you back in to land and back out over the breakers again for another ride. When my turn came, I found it incredibly difficult to get over the break. Every wave that came in just pushed me back or crashed over the top of me, leaving me gasping for breath and very frustrated. Eventually, I made it past wave after wave and lay over the back of the kayak on the flatter water some distance out, resting and regaining some energy.

After a minute or so, basking in the sun, I composed myself, looked around for a suitable wave to bring me in to the shore and paddled as hard as I could to get on board. I missed the first one. I missed the second one. Then, on my third attempt I felt the sheer power of the sea driving me onward. What a feeling! It was pure adrenalin, sensing the enormity of the sea's strength pushing me along. Then it happened. The wave broke over the top of me. No longer was I so thrilled with the force of the water as it now tossed me round and around, deep under the surface, and helped me appreciate how our clothing feels when it is in the washing machine, on the fastest cycle.

I knew there was no way I was rolling back up from this, so I released the kayak's straps from my thighs, kept a good hold of my paddle and allowed my buoyancy aid to raise me to some much appreciated air. That was when I looked frantically around for the boat in the desperate hope I could somehow get back on and paddle again. As Steve watched from the shore to see my little head bobbing up and down, I watched from a long way out to see his kayak parking up on the beach. It was a long swim back, which I shall never forget, not least because I was well aware of the fishermen on the coast casting for hammerhead sharks. Not good! Still, it was fun with a capital "F".

The next day, Steve and I went out again. This time the breakers were even higher. Just like kayaking on the river, the higher the better. Unlike the river, though, you don't simply seal launch off the bank and find yourself in the water. For surf kayaking, as I was learning, you need to work hard to get to a place where you can catch a wave in the first instance. After ten exhausting minutes of trying to get over the breakers I just felt ill. It was the hardest work-out I'd had in a long time. I was not nearly as physically fit as I needed to be, but neither did I possess a good mental attitude. I gave up in order to have a rest, and I said to my paddling partner, "We'll just never get out there today". Steve replied with a comment that really hit me hard, like one of those waves pounding me in the face. "You certainly won't with that attitude."

He was absolutely right, and I knew it. My ego didn't allow me to reveal how much his comment got to me, but it had. "You certainly won't with that attitude." . . . "You certainly won't with that attitude." . . . "You certainly won't with that attitude." The phrase kept going over and over in my head. "Why was I having such negative thinking?" I wondered. "Come on! Get out there", I said to myself. The trouble was, as much as I tried, I never did manage it. I really was exhausted, and the breakers were very powerful.

Was I a failure though? I don't believe so. I was a learner, that's all. I had gained a terrific new experience, a wonderful story to tell and lessons learnt that would hold me in good stead for the next opportunity I had to test my whole body, and mind, at surf kayaking. "When we give ourselves permission to fail, we at the same time give ourselves permission to excel", says Musicologist Eloise Ristad.[91] Whether to succeed or fail, roll on the next time I'm in sunny, warm, beautiful Fernandina Beach!

---

91 Quoted in *Failing Forward* by John C. Maxwell

The point of all these stories and quotations, and points of view, is that life is not a trial run. It is the real thing. We're going to make mistakes along the way. On this river we call life, it is inevitable that we will have waves that overpower us, eddy lines that rock us, holes that threaten to drown us and many an experience of capsize. It's okay. That's the natural way of things. As Ken Whiting says, "No matter how good your balance is, sometimes you will lose it".[92] Maturity on the way means that we'll accept that there will be hard lessons to learn and big mistakes to be made. The lessons that educate us, however, will assist us on the next section of our journey. We don't need to fear capsizing. We need to gain the skills to roll back up, again and again and again. God bless you as you acquire that ability on the water and in life.

---

92 Whiting, Ken and Varette, Kevin, *Whitewater Kayaking*, p. 76

River Rescue

"Christianity is in essence a rescue religion."

John Stott, *The Contemporary Christian*, p. 309

"God sent his Son into the world, not to condemn the world, but to save the world."

Jesus of Nazareth, John 3:17

I once asked a fellow kayaker if he felt that paddling was a team sport. He said "No", but I disagreed. As much as we can learn to paddle and surf and roll as individuals, still, by the inherently dangerous nature of this fabulous recreational activity, there are times when it is going to be incredibly important to not be on the river all on your own. Some time or another, we're going to need some outside help to rescue us, to save us, from very real peril.

Take the following extract from the biography of the late, legendary, Scottish kayaker, Andy Jackson, the events of this story encountered by Jackson's girlfriend, Bridget.

"I was spending large periods of time surfing the hole upside down; I'd get upright and dig for the end of the hole but I wasn't making progress and the loops just kept coming. Upside down again, I needed air; time for the grab loop. I surfaced on the foam pile and saw the rapid ahead and then went deep. I kicked for the surface. One gulp. A rock slid past my vision and I went down again. Two more recircs and I began to feel the pattern. Haven't I seen that rock before? I tried to kick off it as I slid once more into the hole. No one can get to me I thought as I went down for the fourth time. Relax. Try to save air. Down again. I didn't even know I was out until I heard a voice and saw a kayak nearby."[93]

Imagine if Bridget had paddled solo. She could have got into all sorts of very, very serious trouble. As it was, there was a voice to be heard and a kayak to be spotted as she eventually was rescued from the hole she found herself in! Indeed, most of the time, in between gasps for breath and descents into the deep water, she was hoping that one of her party could help her, rescue her, save her.

Champion whitewater kayaker, Ken Whiting, tells his dramatic story of a great escape too! "After a few enjoyable times getting swirl-o-grammed in the whirlpools, things quickly went sour. Like a lemming making its final leap, I hurled myself into the river and was immediately pulled under water . . . with the surface only inches away, the river trolls grabbed my ankles and unmercifully yanked me down into complete darkness. Running out of air, and without any light to guide me to the surface, panic set in swiftly. . . I thought I couldn't hold my breath any longer, until finally, I began swallowing water. The darkness that surrounded me was replaced with an even deeper blackness as I passed out. Moments later, I returned to my senses. . . . Before I knew what was happening, I broke through the surface and was taking the biggest, most welcomed breath

---

93 Cameron, Ronald, *Tall Stories*, pp. 56, 57.

of my life. My buddies were there quickly to tow me ashore, and I dragged my spent body onto the riverbank."[94]

I quote these stories of such physical traumas because they can also become a spiritual experience as those who go through such experiences contemplate what might have been! They lead us to S.O.S. calls where we cry out or blow our emergency whistle in distress. As a church minister it interests me, of course, that the very phrase S.O.S. has spiritual overtones, for it means 'Save Our Souls'. And so, yet again, because there are situations when we are all like this, I'll develop here another wonderful contrast between this sport and Christian spirituality, as this chapter focuses upon our need for rescue or salvation.

At the heart of the Christian faith is the notion that Jesus is the Saviour of the world; the one who 'saves our souls'. Some would have us believe that this central tenant of the Church is a simple and straightforward doctrine, but, alas, it really is not so. "Salvation is a complex notion",[95] says theology Professor, Alister McGrath. Indeed, it is in theology, and it is on rivers. Not only are there specific university courses for trainee ministers on the topic of salvation (or soteriology, to give it the rather grander academic title), but there are also very specific river safety and rescue courses for those who wish to be more competent paddlers too.

Over time, along with a consistently recurring view that salvation merely means winning a place in heaven through Christ's death on the cross, the concept of being 'saved' in church circles has become something of a joke. No doubt you know the kind of thing: Jesus saves, but he couldn't do it on my salary! Such poking of fun comes not least, I am sure, because of the insistence of some street preachers

---

94 Whiting, Ken, *Whitewater Kayaking*, p. 141.
95 McGrath, Alister, *Christian Theology – An Introduction*, p. 337

who yell at passers by, asking them the question, "Are you saved?" Perhaps joking is the kindest way to handle it. I'd make jokes too if some convert to whitewater kayaking decided to stand on a street corner and lambast people for not joining him on the water.

Imagine it! With a river guidebook being waved about in his hand, the new paddling preacher might yell, "I have good news for you today. I once was like you; you who walk on by! All I cared about was spending money and shopping and going about my business. Not now, though! No sir! I have a new life where my eyes have been opened to God's creation once more, where I feel more alive than I've ever been before and, though I have struggled to stay on the right line, I have learnt to paddle better day after day. Oh, I've capsized as you have, over and over again. Oh, I've been lost in the darkness of the cold waters that have chilled me. In fact, I was drowning in the darkness of the waters that engulfed me. But I am here today to tell you, my friend, what you need to know: that a fellow kayaker rescued me, and I'm saved! Hallelujah! You can be too! But will you keep on walking by? Will you miss out on this chance for re-creation? Or will you take up your paddle and follow?"

If I heard a fellow paddler doing this I'd be mortified, as well as think he'd gone just a bit loopy! There are so many better ways of helping people know how many benefits come from our sport – which is why, I guess, I've never actually heard anyone preach on street corners about kayaking! Surely, then, there must be better ways of sharing the good news about the faith as well!

Even if I don't agree with it, though, I do at least understand the reasoning why such forceful, direct, insistent Christian preaching takes place. The preacher, you see, is on a rescue mission that seeks to save people from perishing eternally in the rivers of burning sulphur in hell, which is what he (and it usually is a he) believes will happen if individuals don't have faith in Jesus Christ.

Having been someone who has spent significant amounts of my time studying what it means to be 'saved', I'm afraid that I just don't agree with such a narrow definition of salvation as this idea of the soul being saved from hell when you die. Thankfully, I'm not alone in such thinking. Steve Chalke, author of *The Lost Message of Jesus*, says, "We live with the idea that the gospel's chief aim is to make us fit for heaven, when in reality Jesus' message is focussed on making us citizens and recipients of the Kingdom of God today".[96] Rob Bell repeats the same message in *Love Wins*: "When the gospel is diminished to a question of whether or not a person will 'get into heaven', that reduces the good news to a ticket, a way to get past the bouncer and into the club. The good news is better than that. . . . A discussion about how to 'just get into heaven' has no place in the life of a disciple of Jesus, because it's missing the point of it all".[97] Such an idea of Jesus' mission being one to save us from hell is all too simplistic, and, to repeat Professor McGrath's comment once more: "Salvation is a complex notion".[98]

Level five British Canoe Union coach, and director of the Kayaking Publisher *Pesda Press*, Franco Ferrero, understands that saving someone in a whitewater rescue situation is also 'complex'. In his book, straightforwardly titled *White Water Safety & Rescue*, he says, "The writing of this book started when I tried to put together course notes for the safety and rescue courses I was running at Plas y Brenin. It soon became clear what a huge topic it

---

96 Chalke, Steve and Mann, Alan, *The Lost Message of Jesus*, p. 36
97 Bell, Rob, *Love Wins*, pp. 178, 179
98 McGrath, Alister, *Christian Theology – An Introduction*, p. 337

was. . ." Franco further states, "Whitewater Safety and Rescue can appear a complex subject". [99]

From the principles of safety to dealing with swimmers or pinned boats, or having and using equipment properly, to assessing risk, communicating with those needing rescued and others helping in the rescue, the route to a paddler's salvation on (or more seriously, under) the water requires a book of 298 pages! I could, of course, add the many other resources available in DVDs that we could and should watch, the courses kayakers could and should attend and the practice of particular exercises we could and should involve ourselves within. However, I hope you get my point. If it is not easy or straightforward to rescue someone on the river, it is certainly not an uncomplicated issue to understand how Jesus Christ might save the world.

Equally, even though it remains the predominant view in most churches, salvation does not need to only focus upon one aspect of the Christian narrative: the cross on which Jesus was crucified. I tend to agree with Professor of New Testament Interpretation, Joel Green, on this point: "God's saving act is the incarnation, which encompasses the whole of his life including – but not limited to – his death on the cross".[100] If Revd Dr John Stott is correct in the statement at the outset of this chapter, that "Christianity is in essence a rescue religion",[101] it appears that the working out of what such a statement actually means can have multiple answers and the need for many a discussion. What is for sure is that a further colleague of mine is absolutely correct when he says, "The Church's fixation on the death of Jesus

99 Ferrero, Franco, *White Water Safety & Rescue*, p. 4, 7

100 Tidball, Derek and Hilborn, David (Eds), *The Atonement Debate*, p. 158

101 Stott, John, *The Contemporary Christian*, p. 309

as the universal saving act must end, and the place of the cross must be reimagined in Christian faith. Why? Because of the cult of suffering and the vindictive God behind it".[102]

Don't misunderstand me, please. I appreciate how counter-intuitive this all sounds for any of us who have had any kind of upbringing in the church. What I am saying here really, really clashes with that which we are likely to have heard again and again and again. Let me be clear that, as a church minister, I know very well that, when it comes to Jesus, his very name means "the one who saves" and that he himself is credited as saying that he came "to seek and to save the lost". I know, too, that he is called our Saviour, and that it is a very common belief that his death on the cross saves us from our sins. I know all about the message of his resurrection on that first Easter Sunday and how it offers the hope that we can be saved from eternal death through faith. Yet, the longer I have been journeying down this river of life the more I have realised that this Christ saves me from more than the preoccupations of sin and death and hell. Christ has saved me, and continually offers me rescue, from the rather more tangible hell on earth that I all too easily create for myself time after time!

My faith has saved me from temptations, wrongdoing, stupidity, a broken relationship with God, broken relationships with other people, a broken marriage, being too self-centred, fatigue, being overly materialistic, my own ignorance, resting on my laurels, judging others and – a common thread woven throughout this book – from living a dull, purposeless life of monotony. The good news that Jesus is my Saviour really is excellent news on all sorts of levels, not *just* good news about forgiveness from sin and life after death.

---

102 Jones, Alan, *Reimagining Christianity*, p. 132

So, I've debated salvation is not just about some kind of celestial insurance policy to be cashed in upon reaching our personal river's great estuary. Rather, salvation is about many other very ordinary things that we encounter long before the time comes for us to actually meet our Maker. Whitewater safety and rescue courses and theories are equally not just for the focus on the ultimate worst case scenario: the potential loss of life. There are pinned boats to be saved, lost paddles to be recovered, bone breakages to be prevented. Indeed, there are guiding principles of safety and rescue that we would do well to put in place far away from the danger of death and long before any difficult situation arises.

Boating alone would be one such principle. The river has such a unique and perpetually changing life of its own that, if we think we are able to handle it in a solitary state, we do well to remember those who have not been so fortunate – even with the additional, external assistance of fellow boaters. Regarding my discussion, then, of matters upon the river of life, don't take what I am saying here as fact, and don't just read this book all on your own. Much of what I write is merely *my* thoughtful opinion on the comparisons between kayaking and spirituality. If you are not sure about what I have been saying, then by all means feel free to discuss it with other people whose opinion you trust and respect. Don't ride this river alone either!

Reading the river guidebook is another pre-expedition safety and rescue practice that ought to come as second nature before we venture further upon waterways that we are unfamiliar with. In the guidebook we read about potential hazards, particularly precarious features and common dangers that we do well to avoid. Similarly, as I'll discuss later, the Bible and other sacred texts can be literature that we do well to turn to in order to assess our own journey. We all do ourselves a disservice if we fail to take the time to read and learn, as this can be a magnificent path towards our personal salvation.

Running a river blind has inherent and escalated risks too, so stopping to look all around and to weigh things up for ourselves is always a wise precaution. In Matthew's Gospel Jesus said, "Seek and you shall find" (Matthew 7:7), inviting individuals to use their God-given eyes and ears, feelings and intellect to work out what they believe and why. Later, also, John the Baptist sent his disciples to ask Jesus if he really was the Messiah. Jesus responded, "Go back and report to John what you hear and see" (Matthew 11:4). He was saying not to just have blind faith, but believe, in part, because of what is observed. Openly and honestly assessing our observations on the literal or metaphorical river can only increase confidence.

I, for one, do not encourage faith that is blind. In fact, I happen to like what Derren Brown, that baffling and wonderfully entertaining U.K. illusionist, says in his book, *Tricks of the Mind*. "The brave or intelligent Christian who is interested in questioning blind faith would be well advised to read Richard Dawkins book *The God Delusion* . . . perhaps even with a view to strengthening their own belief." I agree wholeheartedly. Indeed, I have read Dawkins book in great detail and have quoted from it already in this text. Fellow Christians may criticise such practise, but I advise not to be afraid of varied opinion. Take the risk of reading Dawkins if he's not your usual reading material. Similarly, take the risk of reading Jesus of Nazareth if he is not usually on your reading list. Such activity is called 'scouting', you see, and it gives us the very thing that is essential to every kayaker: great balance.[103]

---

103 I can recommend Alister McGrath's, *The Dawkins Delusion* and David Robertson's *The Dawkins Letters*

All in all, the concept of Salvation has various aspects to it, whether in the church or in the canoe club. To say that my fellow kayakers have saved me from death is to put it all too crudely and melodramatically. To say that Jesus has saved me from sin and eternal damnation is to put it too stereotypically. In fact, not only does it become all too prescriptive about what the term 'salvation' means, but it actually misinterprets biblical teaching on the subject and rejects centuries of Christian tradition!

According to Eddie Gibbs and Ryan Bolger, "The Gospel, as proclaimed by Jesus Christ and as understood by the early church, was always more than simply a message of personal salvation and, even more narrowly, the way to get to heaven when one dies".[104] Christ came to save the world, not just individual human beings and their souls, and such salvation includes saving people from starvation and exploitation, saving the panda from extinction, and saving the world from environmental disaster, amongst other things. "For God so loved the *world* that he sent his only son. . ." (John 3:16).

That favourite author of mine, Brian McLaren, says it well, I think: "For people who come from evangelical and fundamentalist backgrounds (as I do), life is about being or getting saved, and knowing it. . . . I sometimes think we jump to that interpretation of *salvation* too quickly – and in so doing we miss the full point of salvation".[105]

This is not to take away from the fact that Jesus Christ does offer to rescue human beings from death through the hope of resurrection and from all our cumulative sin through the unconditional love, mercy and grace of God. However, what I write here and what the authors I quote

---

104 Gibbs, Eddie and Bolger, Ryan K., *Emerging Churches*, p. 48

105 McLaren, Brian D. and Campolo, Tony, *Adventures in Missing the Point*, p. 19, 21

do is to *add* to a wider sense of holistic salvation, rather than a narrower, individualistic rescue.

It is true that "The master theme of the Christian gospel is salvation", as J. I. Packer writes, but note that he goes on to say, "Salvation is a picture-word of *wide application* that expresses the idea of rescue from jeopardy and misery into a state of safety"[106] (emphasis mine). The meaning of salvation is as wide as the widest section of life's river. As missiologist David Bosch also says, "Salvation is as coherent, broad, and deep as the needs and exigencies of human existence".[107]

I like that phrase "broad and deep". It resonates with those of us who like being on the water paddling. Indeed, it echoes what was said in the very opening chapter of this book when I quoted expert kayaker, Ken Whiting: "Whitewater kayaking is much more than just a physical activity. . . . It will in myriad ways challenge you, strengthen you, reward you, connect you, mystify you, and, most importantly, free you".[108] The Christian doctrine of Salvation will also challenge, strengthen, reward, connect, mystify and free us. It is not a science that has been proven, or even a doctrine that has been universally agreed. Rather, like the river, it has to do with Jesus back in Bible times, our lives right now and the life that we yet shall experience in our immortality.

Again, professor of Systematic Theology, Alistair McGrath, says, "The Christian understanding of Salvation presupposes that something *has* happened, that something *is now* happening and that something *further will still*

---

106 Packer, James I., *Concise Theology*, p. 146
107 Bosch, David, *Transforming Mission*, p. 400
108 Whiting, Ken and Varette, Kevin, *Whitewater Kayaking – The Ultimate Guide*, p. ix

happen to believers". [109] Maybe it helps to try and imagine this as a kayaker on an expedition part way down a river. We know where we've paddled already, we may be pretty sure of where we are now, yet we know that there still is more to come. Being 'saved' in Christian terms is not something we can possibly know about completely, for if there is part of it that has to do with being saved for life eternal, we cannot possibly know about that aspect completely until the time comes when we are no longer here as we are currently!

This, though, remains the problem for many of my kayaking and non-kayaking friends outwith the church. The myth remains strong that this is what the church is all about; that there are those destined for the heavenly realm and others who are on a fast track to fire and brimstone. Please, please, please, I appeal to you, that this is not at all what this particular paddling padre believes or preaches.

I, along with Rob Bell, understand only too well the concerns any thinking person has about such theological scaremongery. "This is from an actual church website: 'The unsaved will be separated forever from God in hell.' This is from another: 'Those who don't believe in Jesus will be sent to eternal punishment in hell.' And this is from another: 'The unsaved dead will be committed to an eternal conscious punishment.' . . . The people experiencing this separation and punishment will feel all of it, we are told, because they'll be fully conscious of it, fully awake and aware of every single second of it, as it never lets up for billions and billions of years. All this on a website. Welcome to our church."[110]

---

109 McGrath, Alister, *Christian Theology – An Introduction*, p. 341
110 Bell, Rob, *Love Wins*, pp. 95, 96

A number of years ago I took our youth group to a Christian activity centre where the teenagers in our care could go mountain-biking, horse-riding and, wait for it, kayaking! At the end of each tiring, action-packed day we would have our well-earned dinner, followed by some time out to listen to one of the centre's staff speaking to their visitors about some aspect of the Christian faith. On one occasion, as the speaker enthused about faith in Jesus, he went on to make the point that we all need to make a decision as to whether we will follow him or not. More than this, he went on to say that following Christ is all about what will happen to us when we die. Know Jesus and heaven is the destination. Ignore Jesus and you're headed for the place of everlasting fire. Apart from that outlook jarring with my own thinking, I became completely repulsed by the next comment that was forced upon the young people whose parents had entrusted to my leadership for a couple of days. "If you're travelling home after this weekend and your minibus crashes, and some of you die, where is it that you are going to end up if you don't know Jesus?" was the overly zealous challenge.

Sadly, such a situation arises from that extreme focus upon the violence and drama of Christ's crucifixion, as if that one act is his sole saving act. Again, then, we can do worse than hear from some authors who have thought much about the subject but come to a quite different conclusion. "The saving work of Christ is the outcome of his total career", says Nigel Wright in *The Radical Evangelical*, "And though it may be focussed peculiarly in the cross this should not eclipse its full scope". [111] Similarly, Marcus Borg in his book *The Heart of Christianity* says, " 'Jesus died for our sins' was originally a subversive metaphor,

---

111 Wright, Nigel, *The Radical Evangelical*, p. 60

not a literal description of either God's purpose or Jesus' vocation. It was a metaphorical proclamation of radical grace; and properly understood, it still is".[112]

Going back to my experience at the Christian activity camp, as it happens, I was appalled by the forceful insistence that the young minds be made up there and then. I made an official complaint and was promptly told that maybe I shouldn't bring my group to a Christian camp if I didn't want the youngsters to hear the gospel. The gospel? The very word 'gospel' means 'good news', but this rendition of it didn't sound like very good news to me! 'Turn or burn' is the way I've heard it put before, and I cannot pretend for a moment to be impressed by such forms of evangelism. Frankly, I don't believe there is any need for such pressurised demands for on-the-spot decision making like this – let alone worrying teenagers with the possibility of imminent death.

On the river, any good coach will understand the need to minimise fear and panic in a rescue situation. It seems to me to be counter-productive to increase these very things in any talk of the eternal rescue of our souls when we preach about salvation. Anyway, we don't need to terrorise individuals for a conversion or allegiance to the Christian faith. "To know Jesus is not an event, a ritual, a creed, a religion. It is a journey of trust and adventure".[113]

Ah, once more we have those beautiful words "journey" and "adventure"; words that kayakers are very comfortable with. Jesus, the Saviour, is our companion for the trip. He'll save us when we get to the end of the river, yes. However, he'll *also* save us time and again on the way, for

112 Borg, Marcus, *The Heart of Christianity – Rediscovering a Life of Faith*, Harper One, New York, 2004, p. 95

113 Gibbs, Eddie and Bolger, Ryan K., *Emerging Churches*, p. 47

the jeopardy and misery that many people face is right here and now, not only in the life to come!

Brian McLaren, again, agrees: "Here's the ancient Jewish way of missing the point (thinking salvation is only about politics in the here and now) and the modern Christian way of missing the point (thinking salvation is only about escaping hell when you die). There's another approach: that salvation means being rescued from fruitless ways of life here and now, to share in God's saving love for all creation, in an adventure called the kingdom of God, the point of which you definitely don't want to miss".[114]

I'm hoping that *we'll* not miss the point as we seek our adventure of living. If the Lord's prayer is correct, then we need to pray sincerely, "Thy kingdom come *on earth* as it is in heaven". (Or, for that matter, "Thy kingdom come *on the water* as it is in heaven".) Such thinking means asking that God's Kingdom of love, grace, mercy, peace, and salvation might come to us here and now, as well as in the afterlife. I, for one, say "amen" to that. Couldn't we all do with a world saved from its brokenness, divisions and trouble? We need each other as fellow paddlers. We need each other as fellow pilgrims. We need each other as fellow human beings on this amazing journey of life. And all of us, together, are dependent upon our God. Maybe he will not just save the Queen, but save us all – from ourselves. We're all, too often, in need of rescue!

---

114 McLaren, Brian D. and Campolo, Tony. *Adventures in Missing the Point*, p. 25

LIVING WATER

"See the rivers how they run
Through the woods and meads, in shade and sun,
Sometimes swift, sometimes slow –
Wave succeeding wave, they go. . ."

John Dyer[115]

In the New Testament, Jesus talks of himself in many symbols and metaphors. If he is not referring to himself as "The Good Shepherd" (John 10:11), he is calling himself "The Bread of Life" (John 6:35). Other times he will ask us to use our imaginations as he says, "I am the light of the world" (John 8:12) or, again, "I am the Vine" (John 15:1). In regard to the theme of this book, there are two other concepts that Christ uses to help us appreciate that he is our companion on the journey of life. Firstly, he calls himself, "The Way" (John 14:6) and, secondly, the "Living water" (John 4:14).

I suppose that the description of Jesus as "The Way" is entirely appropriate for us to consider as kayakers, as we follow the route of a river and find ourselves proceeding along the way that the current will naturally take us. Still, for me, the concept of Jesus as "The living water" is even more apt for a book about the spirituality of whitewater

---

115 Quoted in *Peace Like a River* by Donny Finley, p. 18

kayaking. If ever there was something unique about this sport, and the surface upon which it is practised, it is the fact that the water is not motionless or stationary, but is fluid and active. 'The way' could refer to a road or a path, but 'living water' is more specifically about a stream or creek or brook. As Jeff Imbach correctly says in *The River Within*, "There is a great difference between a path and a river. A path is static; a river is dynamic. A path is passive; a river will find a way".[116]

Jeff is not the only author I have read who has reflected on the vigorous nature of the river in terms of how it flows and 'lives'. In his book, *The Rock and the River*, Martin Thornton clarifies the difference very well, highlighting how close this non-static character of waterways is to the ongoing, changeable nature of the Christian faith. "The obvious thing about a river is that it moves, it sparkles and splashes, it is never still, never the same from one moment to another. Sometimes it meanders dreamily through the meadows, sometimes it broadens into a placid loch, sometimes it hurtles down the hillside in a roaring torrent. It represents the dynamic element in the Christian tradition: it is ascetical, or spiritual, or practical theology." [117]

A practical theology is something I hope to live by, and hope to share with others, for sometimes the very notion of any theological discourse congers up a more negative thinking of high-browed academics in ivory towers. There the discussion might range around pneumatology, eschatology, soteriology and epistemology – or any number of other 'ologies' that most people, day to day, would never likely deliberate. Theology itself, indeed, without getting into the finer nuances, is probably a topic that many will

---

116 Imbach, Jeff, *The River Within*, p. 262
117 Thornton, Martin, *The Rock and the River*, p. 13

even think has nothing to do with them at all. Have *you*, for instance, described yourself as a theologian recently?

Strangely, though, "Everyone is a theologian", as Tony Campolo asserts in his co-authored book, *Adventures in Missing the Point*.[118] Anytime that any of us say something like, "I believe in God" or "I don't believe in God" we are stating our opinion about the deity. By default, we are engaging in theological comment. As Sinclair Ferguson and David Wright explain in the preface to their *New Dictionary of Theology*, "The root meaning of 'theology' is 'speaking about God'".[119]

The above is all by way of putting the rest of this chapter into proper context, for here I'd like to think of Jesus as that, 'Living Water', and help us appreciate that, if he did not describe himself as a stationary pool, or a still loch, then there is scope to understand that what we believe about him will be constantly on the move; evolving, developing and moving as living water does.

To me, this is a very interesting and very important thing. In church circles, and outwith, there are some people who seem to think that belief in God is a kind of yes or no issue, for which you are either in or you are out. It's as if there are certain doctrines and dogmas which, if you believe them, mean that you are a Christian. If you don't believe them then, ipso facto, you are not part of the flock. I, however, don't buy that.

My theological understanding, for instance, has changed a lot throughout the years in which I have believed. When I first came to faith my beliefs were rather simplistic, based upon the very limited knowledge I had at that time

118 McLaren, Brian D. and Campolo, Tony, *Adventures in Missing the Point*, p. 31

119 Ferguson, Sinclair B. and Wright, David W., *New Dictionary of Theology*, p. vii

of church history, varying theological points of view and my personal experience of church life. As I, myself, have changed, with hundreds more grey hairs on my head and a few more wrinkles on my face, my understanding of God has also developed in new ways. As pastor, author and TV presenter, Steve Chalke has said, "God's work is an ongoing task in each person's life".[120]

It is just the same with kayaking, or any new life skill we might try and develop. We move from ignorance to novice status, then, if we put in the time and effort, move from intermediate to expert. All the way along we are guided into new truths, new insight, and new experience. Our understanding changes and fluctuates according to the new ideas we are able to take onboard, and, as a result, we change too.

Jesus, himself, realised that he wasn't going to be able to address every topic and enlighten humanity on every single subject during his three short years of ministry. That's why, in the Gospel of St. John, chapter 16 verses 12 and 13 he says, "I have much more to say to you, more than you can now bear. But when he, the Spirit of truth, comes he will guide you into all truth. He will not speak on his own; he will speak only what he hears, and he will tell you what is yet to come".

"Yet to come"; this is living water in action. Look upstream. No matter how many millions or billions of gallons of water have flowed right past the spot where you are paddling, there is always more yet to come! A river is not static, but always flowing and progressing; it is always in motion. If any faith that we possess is a living faith, a vibrant faith, a dynamic faith, then it will, by default, be an unfinished faith. Sadly, faith which declares 'the truth'

---

120 Chalke, Steve and Mann, Alan, *The Lost Message of Jesus*, p. 145

as a once-and-for-all, unwavering conviction is really no faith at all. It is, rather, a dogmatic declaration of certainty which is quite the opposite of the very definition of the word 'faith'.

Our understanding of God and our development of belief must always be in a constant state of 'becoming'. As Brian McLaren states in his book, *The Church on the Other Side*, "We don't expect anyone at long last to paint 'the right painting' or to finally complete scientific inquiry with the last discovery. Yet somehow we have thought that theologians either had or were about to finish theology – cross the final t and correct the final misconception – as if God were a more limited realm than science or art!"[121]

In many ways, this book is just a living part of my personal, ongoing journey and the development of my faith. It is only a personal attempt to reflect upon my kayaking hobby, in which I have sensed new insights about God and myself. Seeing the world from a water-based rather than a land-based perspective, my head and heart have been opened to new sensations that inspire and challenge previous assumptions. I love it just as much as the first disciples must have loved following Jesus towards the new ideas and territories into which he led them.

Such thinking takes us back to my previous chapter on the subject of risk. Most of us prefer dealing in certainties. We don't want to rock the boat and have our precious traditions and predispositions unsettled. It can be challenging and uncomfortable, or it can even be frightening. But I'm a whitewater kayaker, remember! Rocking the boat comes naturally. In fact, rocking the boat is an essential skill whereby if you don't edge from one side to the other, going with the flow of the river, that same river will

---

121 McLaren, Brian D., *The Church on the Other Side*, p. 66

surprise you often and capsize you again and again. If we want a vibrant, sustainable faith that moves with the flow of God's Spirit, we are going to need to take the risk of acknowledging that we don't know it all yet – and, indeed, never shall.

Movement and flow within our belief systems should not threaten us; they should excite us. It is a persistent adventure of working and re-working out who this God is in whom we profess belief. As, again, Martin Thornton says, "I would rather watch the modern disturbance in the river, preferring it to conventional placidity and acknowledging that, despite a certain invigorating danger, it is easier to swim with a strong current than to wade through a stagnant swamp; even an orthodox one".[122]

The river never stands still. It may say in Hebrews 13:8 that "Jesus is the same yesterday, today and forever", but because *we* are always changing, our understanding and interpretation of who this same Jesus is will always be adapting to the developed insights we gain along the way. The sixteenth-century Spanish mystic, St John of the Cross, puts it like this in his classic, *The Dark Night of the Soul*: "The soul never remains static as it travels on the road of contemplation as it is always rising or falling".[123] We just need to exchange the word 'road' for 'river' and we can appreciate this very traditional comment in our contemporary thinking without problem.

In fact, such ideas were not new in the sixteenth century and are not new ideas now. Written between 300 and 700 BC, the Old Testament book of Job states, "God is above and beyond our understanding" (Job 36:26). That was true then and is still true now! God, by definition, cannot be anything other than that which is beyond the

---

122 Thornton, Martin, *The Rock and the River*, p. 16
123 St John of the Cross, *The Dark Night of the Soul*, p. 98

possibilities of our thinking. To be otherwise is to apportion the status of God to ourselves. What makes us think that we might be able to contain him in specific or conclusive doctrines and theologies now? "We are the river. The river is flowing, and yet it is always in the process of becoming even as it moves towards its destination, the sea."[124]

In the day to day of life it is so easy to forget these things. Without thinking and rethinking who we are, and what we believe, we can come to particular decisions at one stage or another, sticking with those choices, and even defending them when challenged by new information or enlightenment. To not change and adapt our beliefs according to new scientific, cultural, theological or recreational input is to plod wearily through life. More exciting, purposeful, meaningful life can't accept such blandness. To quote John Ortberg one last time, "When life is on spiritual autopilot, rivers of living water do not flow through it with energy and joy".[125]

I want a life with energy and joy, so taking time to engage with our deeper questions and doubts can be much more of an adventurous route to paddle. There we experience the wave train of high eureka moments and low troughs of confusion. The waters will sometimes appear crystal clear, and at other times seem very muddied indeed. Yet through it all our mixed and meandering reflections mirror the beloved river in its constant yet variable flow. The river is a living body of water, just as Jesus describes himself as living water too. Personal faith in this Christ, then, will naturally be fluid and unpredictable. Don't settle for anything less.

---

124 Smith Jr, Archie, *Navigating the Deep River*, p. 87
125 Ortberg, John, *If You Want to Walk on Water You've Got to Get Out of the Boat*, p. 37

THE RIVER GUIDEBOOK

"Scripture is the truth that we live by, our authoritative guidebook as we Ride the River."

Larry Christenson, *Ride the River*, p. 103

As I've mentioned before, the Bible is full of rivers from beginning to end. Indeed, flowing all the way through the pages of the Old and New Testaments are mentions of waterways that obviously were important for all sorts of economic, sanitary, trading and spiritual purposes. So, when we read the Bible it doesn't take long before we come across references to the Euphrates or the Jordan or the Nile.

It is not long in life, either, before we shall come across a reference to the Bible as well. "Can the Leopard change his spots?" (Jeremiah 13:23), "The salt of the earth" (Matthew 5:13), "An eye for an eye" (Matthew 5:38), "Go the extra mile" (Matthew 5:41), "No rest for the wicked" (Isaiah 57:20) – these, amongst many more common phrases, are all biblical texts utilised in everyday life.

Even in kayaking circles, parallels are drawn with this wonderful sport and ancient stories and phrases from scripture. Lito Tejada-Flores, for instance, in his book *Wildwater*, draws upon biblical content as he describes the challenge, wonder and dynamism of the journey down a river in a small boat. "With a kayak you play a kind of David-and-Goliath game against elemental river forces in a light, elegant, and seemingly fragile craft, making your peace with foaming waters, sudden drops and curling waves."[126]

Doug Ammons also twice refers to the good book when he says, firstly, "You can float down the main tongue, or you can search for the river's secrets. Seek and ye shall find" [127] (Matthew 7:7). Secondly, Ammons quotes the golden rule when he says, "The fact is, if you want a good partner, then we'd better be one ourselves"[128] (Matthew 7:12).

In Scotland, my homeland, referring to the Bible as the "good book", as I just have, offers an even more interesting spin on this latest kayaking metaphor I present because, where we refer to lakes as 'lochs' and streams as 'burns', we also refer to the good book as the 'guid book'. Simply add the second vowel in our alphabet and what have you got? You've got the guid book that *is* a guide book!

Are these the only tenuous links I can make between this aspect of Christian faith and that of the river though? Not at all! In fact, this is one of the chapters of this book that has almost written itself. The strength of familiarity I feel in regard to both my passion for kayaking and my zeal for God is probably most clearly revealed in the concept of a river guidebook and the Bible as a guidebook for life. As St Thomas Aquinas said many centuries ago, "Revelation comes in two volumes, Nature and the Bible".[129] For me it is specifically the river and the Bible.

126 Tejada-Flores, Lito, *Wildwater*, p. 10
127 Ammons, Doug, *Whitewater Philosophy*, p. 16
128 Ammons, Doug, *Whitewater Philosophy*, p. 21
129 Quoted in *One River, Many Wells* by Matthew Fox, p. 49

Not quite as long ago as Aquinas, William Neil authored a little book called *The Plain Man Looks at the Bible*. In that slim volume he wrote, "The Bible offers a certain interpretation of life and asks us to make up our minds one way or the other".[130] Immediately upon reading this, I realised that this is exactly what a river guidebook does too; it offers a certain interpretation of waterways and asks us to make up our minds one way or another about which line to take down them. The guidebook doesn't *command* us to follow a particular line, nor does it demand that we play on a particular wave, or that we absolutely *must* run each section. A guidebook does exactly what it says on the cover: it guides. The Bible is the same.

My hunch, however, is that some of my friends in the church will want to contest my view here, saying that the Ten Commandments, for instance, were not called the ten suggestions. Correct. There are, indeed, areas of the Bible that are to be taken as commands rather than ideas or propositions, but not every single word, sentence, paragraph and chapter. Just like the river, different sections have different features and characteristics.

The Bible contains parts known as the law, and other areas that are poetry, philosophy, hymns of praise, history, letters to the early church and wisdom literature, as well as the Gospels which are in a whole genre all of their own. There are areas of scripture that are general overviews of what biblical characters experienced, how they responded to their circumstances and inferences of how we, too, could respond likewise in similar situations. We don't need to take every word as literally true. On the more progressive wing of the church, Professor Marcus Borg makes the point that, "Contemporary biblical literal-

---

130 Neil, William, *The Plain Man Looks at the Bible*, p. 108.

ism – with its emphasis on biblical infallibility, historical factuality, and moral and doctrinal absolutes – is an obstacle for millions of people".[131] It needn't be so, however. As Rick Warren, pastor of one of America's biggest and more theologically conservative churches says, "The Bible is the comprehensive *guide*book for living the Christian life"[132] (my emphasis).

"It is important to remember that a guidebook's function is to give a rough idea of what we are in for. It is not supposed to be a substitute for our eyes, ears, brain and river sense."[133] So says Franco Ferrero in his publication, *White Water Safety and Rescue*. Again, I see the parallel with scripture. All too often, in my experience, many believers simply declare, "The Bible says . . ." Well, yes, of course it does. That's what books do: say things. But the Bible is not meant to be a substitute for our (God-given) eyes, ears, brain and common sense too!

For starters, the Bible is not really even a book at all; it is a whole library of several different books and letters woven magnificently together through many changing times, in several different geographical areas, by several different people, facing many different situations. As Mike Riddell has argued, "To approach the Bible as a book is to misapprehend it. It may exist between covers; it may contain sheets of paper with words printed upon them; it may have pages which are numbered sequentially. But here the similarities end. . . . It is a collection of bits. . ." and these bits ". . . come from all over the place, and span at least 4000 years of history".[134]

---

131 Borg, Marcus, *The Heart of Christianity*, Harper One, New York 2003, p. 43

132 Warren, Rick, *Bible Study Methods*, p. 9

133 Ferrerro, Franco, *White Water Safety and Rescue*, p. 42

134 Riddell, Mike, *God's Homepage*, pp. 16, 24, 25

Given that we are talking about work that was in existence many, many centuries before the printing press was even dreamt about, let alone thought about, let alone actually invented, let alone utilised, isn't it fascinating that the Bible had a style of production that was quite remarkable for its time – an incredible team effort you could say? It's interesting to me, at least, that in referring to *Scottish Whitewater*, the river guidebook for the land in which I am proud to have been born, Ronald Cameron also states, "The book itself was a remarkable team effort. . ."[135] The guid book and the guide book really do appear to be very similar!

Certain paddlers run rivers for the first time, or at least the first recorded time. They then document some articulated thoughts on the experience they have had and they share those thoughts with others. Those who later come down that same stretch of water are then enabled to gain at least a little insight into what they are likely to experience and to work out how best to address the challenges they too shall face. Of course, no two runs will ever be the same because of changing levels, the different boats being used, the experience and skills of the individual and the line eventually taken. However, there will be enough information and experience shared by the person who took the time to document their first trip, so that future paddlers need not feel they are running things blind!

Similarly, scripture is full of words of wisdom from many a man and woman who has paddled life's river before us. As Susan Saint Sing helpfully records in her book *Spirituality of Sport*, "The path is already laid out by those who have gone before; they experienced the same difficulties, wrestled with the same questions. Their discoveries can lead

---

135 Cameron, Ronald, *Tall Stories*, p. 91

us if we choose to follow".[136] So, scripture tells of times when the flow was high and rough, when many capsized and even perished on the way and what others managed to do to avoid a swim through certain rapids. It tells, also, of how God's peace was found in the calm.

The fact remains that the writers of the various books of the Bible all had different experiences, lived in different cultures, had different personalities and expectations, just like the writers of any book about rivers and their features. It is up to each of us, many centuries on, to read this excellent guidebook for life with a critical, yet trusting eye, all the time knowing that much of the text will mean something different to us than it would have to its early readership.

I'm surprised that many will be surprised by what I am about to say as a minister of the church, but you can't easily read the Bible and take it *all* literally. A.J. Jacobs found this out. He is an agnostic Jew from New York who wrote a book called *The Year of Living Biblically*. If the Bible said, "'Do not cut the hair at the sides of your head or clip off the edges of your beard" (Leviticus 19:27), this author would obey. If it said, "But all creatures in the seas or streams that do not have fins and scales . . . you are to detest" (Leviticus 11:10), then mussels and shrimp are taken off the menu. If the Bible says that we are to 'stone adulterers' (Deuteronomy 22:23,25), so A.J. Jacobs throws little tiny pebbles at his pals, and strangers, whom he learns are not living the most faithful of lives! However, as this particular author tries to abide by all the hundreds of biblical rules and regulations, he makes an interesting observation. "When it comes to the Bible, there is always

---

136 Saint Sing, Susan, *Spirituality of Sport*, p. 12

– but always – some level of interpretation, even on the most seemingly basic of rules."[137]

Someone who knows a great deal about the need for interpretation of scripture is Gene Robinson, the controversial bishop of New Hampshire, USA. Gene is controversial because, as well as being a senior churchman, he is also an openly practising homosexual. In some church circles there are those who believe this is a contradiction and that Gene Robinson has utterly abandoned the pages of scripture as any authoritative text in his life. This simply is not true though. In his book, *In the Eye of the Storm*, Bishop Robinson writes, "The Bible is a collection of many accounts of what it's like to encounter the Living God. Are those words holy? Absolutely. Are they inspired? I believe they are. But are they inerrant? I don't believe so. Because the people who authored those accounts are not inerrant".[138] I agree with this analysis.

"Obey thy mother and father." It sounds straightforward, right? But what does obey actually mean? Do absolutely every single thing that your parents tell you, even if what they tell you isn't the most sensible thing, or if what they demand is against the law? Equally, there is need for interpretation with the words "mother" or "father". If I happen to be born to one woman who has put me up for adoption, and I have lived with my adoptive mother for years, what do I do when I later learn who my biological mother is? Similar issues can arise with dads as well of course. Which mother or father do I obey?

The Bible may be black text printed on a white page, but the issues sometimes have a whole range of grey. Jesus, my goodness, said, "If your right eye causes you to sin,

137 Jacobs, A.J., *The Year of Living Biblically*, p. 19
138 Robinson, Gene, *In the Eye of the Storm*, p. 55

take it out and throw it away", and "If your right hand causes you to sin, cut it off and throw it away" (Matthew 5:29,30). Well, even amongst some Christians who believe that the whole Bible *is* to be taken literally, there seems to be a degree of interpretation for I've never seen a great demand in church circles for eye patches or prosthetics! This is all nothing to be concerned about as scripture is a *guide*book.

The Bible was not written by ancient holy men who sat at a typewriter as God dictated from the clouds what they were to record! Inspired by God, undoubtedly, people wrote down their experiences and insights about the real encounters they had and they passed these insights down to succeeding generations. Over time these texts were laboriously reproduced, again and again, and so we have the pages of these ancient texts in as original a format as is possible, given that we are talking here of thousands of years worth of material. There's no question that scripture contains great mystery, but that too is okay. As Thomas à Kempis said around five centuries ago, "In silence and quietness the devout soul makes progress and learns the hidden mysteries of the scriptures".[139]

I love the story about this actually; the one about the monk who was hidden away in his cell to transcribe, by hand, page after page of the ancient words. One day he was privileged not just to copy a copy of a copy, but to work from one of the very, very earliest of papyrus fragments. Upon reading he began to cry inconsolably. "What's wrong my dear brother in Christ?" asked the abbot. "Has the great depth of the holy word touched your heart in a powerful and awe-inspiring way?" "No", sobbed the celibate monk. "The original says *celebrate*"!

---

139 Thomas à Kempis, *The Imitation of Christ*, p. 51

Then there's the belief that only some particular monks were authorised to be transcribers of the Bible at all. You simply weren't permitted to be a *copier* at all, unless you were a *Canon* or a *Brother*! Sorry!

With humour, serious study, and a good dose of common sense, we work our way through these words of great depth, choosing for ourselves what line to follow. Steadily we can understand that amazingly, miraculously, fantastically, like those of so many eras before us, "Through the words of men we hear the word of God", as said by a dear local colleague, former Moderator of the General Assembly of the Church of Scotland, and a former chaplain to Her Majesty Queen Elizabeth II, the Very Revd Dr Jim Simpson.[140]

No two writers of a section of river will summarise their experience exactly the same. In fact, it is good that they don't for there are no two paddlers who read the guidebook's notes who will experience the run as anyone else has! So it is with scripture: "The Bible has proved adequate to whole lifetimes of exploration. Just when you think you've got it sussed, it takes you off into some previously un-travelled territory".[141]

Isn't that one of the reasons we kayak – the fact that, even on the most familiar of rivers, the features are always surprising us. I can, likewise, read a passage of the Bible one hundred times and still, within those self same verses, find a little nugget of truth that I just had never noticed before. Far from being a dull book of monotony, it is a rich mine of inspiration and guidance.

Even in an atheistic world, the Bible appears to have merit. Of all people, even professor Richard Dawkins recommends it! In his pretty vitriolic diatribe of a book

140 Simpson, J.A., *There is a Time to . . .* p. 71
141 Riddell, Mike, *God's Homepage*, p. 27

called *The God Delusion*, Dawkins says, "An atheistic world-view provides no justification for cutting the Bible, and other sacred texts, out of our education".[142] On this point I agree entirely with a man who thinks I am deluded!

The Bible has influenced our laws, teaches wonderful ethical truths, has some of the most beautiful passages within it and is of great, ongoing significance to a world looking for direction. A Facebook friend of mine, Professor John Drane, who very kindly wrote the foreword for this work with his wife, Olive, puts it this way: "The basic foundation for the western way of life was constructed from the beliefs and purposes of Christianity. The Bible has had a formative influence in the evolution of our legal systems, our morals, our concepts of human rights and our education. Like it or not, none of us can escape from its pervasive influence".[143]

That is just so true! Look at this example; a few bullet points from *Scottish Whitewater.*

"Your main responsibilities are to:

- Care for the environment
- Take responsibility for your own actions
- Respect the interests of other people." [144]

Could you get clearer instruction than if you were reading from the Bible itself?

- "Care for the environment". All I need to do is quote from, perhaps, the most famous verse of all, John 3:16. "For God so loved the world that he sent his only Son . . ." It's not, 'God so loved human beings' or 'God so

142 Dawkins, Richard, *The God Delusion*, p. 387
143 Drane, John, *The Bible: Fact or Fantasy?* p. 14
144 Thomas, Bridget (Ed), *Scottish Whitewater*, p. 8

loved human souls'. It is "God so loved the *world*". To me the world means 'the world'. Human beings, animals (including endangered species), the ozone layer, flora and fauna, the polar icecap, and our beloved rivers!

- "Take responsibility for your own actions". A famous and humorous story from Luke 6 is one place to look for this when Christ speaks to those wanting to ignore their responsibilities and judge others and theirs. "How can you say to your brother, 'Brother, let me take the speck out of your eye,' when you yourself fail to see the plank in your own eye? You hypocrite, first take the plank out of your eye, and then you will see clearly to remove the speck from your brother's eye" (Luke 6:42). Take responsibility for your own actions.

- Respect the interests of other people. That's simply, the Golden rule mentioned already to, "Do unto others as you want others to do unto you" (Matthew 7:12).

All of this was in the guid book before it was in the guide-book. The Bible runs through us all whether we realise it or not, like a river running through a city whether people paddle it or ignore it.

We do well not to dam up its flow, like some hydro scheme blocking the flow of our liquid playgrounds. When we look into these holy pages, and reflect upon them time and again, it can be just as if we were looking at ourselves in the reflection of still water. Again, as my local colleague, Jim Simpson, has said, "The biblical characters walk our streets. Their temperaments, problems and questions are ours".[145] Those biblical characters paddle our rivers too.

Do you wish to learn about love? Turn to the unparalleled 1 Corinthians 13. Are you fearful of death? Look up the ageless Psalm 23. Do you believe in evolution? Turn to

---

145 Simpson, J.A., *There is a Time to . . .,* p. 70.

the opening verses of Genesis and read a magnificent, non-scientific, hymn of praise which documents the unfolding periods of creation that is way, way, ahead of its time. It is, as I've said, no exact scientific documentation – nor was it ever intended to be so – but the Genesis account tells us that the created order had a particular beginning and that it took specific periods of time to develop into all that is. What is so different here from the initiating big bang and the process of evolution?

Some may really struggle with my thinking above. Such a point of view seems to contest centuries of religious belief. That's not new either, however. The Copernican revolution, for one example, rocked the church to the core. As the flow of the river of life continues on its course throughout the generations, it is surely inevitable that each new age will make new discoveries. These same new generations require to interpret scripture according to the new insights gained along the way.

I fully appreciate that the Bible can be a difficult book at times, and that there are many awkward passages that are hard to understand and even harder to put into practice. That doesn't make the book irrelevant; just challenging. Anyone who has ever attempted learning to Eskimo roll will know just how difficult it is, mentally and physically, to work through the component parts of that 180 degree turnaround! Just because something might seem strange to begin with doesn't mean that, with effort at understanding, it might not actually be of immense relevance and use in time.

I don't take my kayak to the rubbish dump just because it doesn't seem to edge or roll or surf as well as the same model does for other paddlers. In recognising that it is me, not the boat that needs attention, I adjust the way I am paddling, I seek advice from those more experienced than myself, I read up on how to manage this boat more ably and then I begin to experience that it can edge, it can roll, it can surf. Our reading of the Bible is really not so different.

Funnily enough, you can study a river guidebook for all you're worth, but this will do you no good if what you are seeking is, for example, information about the space shuttle's last voyage into space! Each book has a specific purpose that needs to be approached in a particular way, and we do well to try and understand what it is we are reading if we want to get the best out of the material before us. I say it again: the Bible is a *guide*book not a scientific, academic textbook. Never has been, never will be!

As pastor Bill Hybels has said, "You can hardly read a page in the Bible without encountering a situation where God is guiding someone. . . . Even Jesus sought guidance!"[146] Why not us, then? After all, "It's the life that counts, not the reading about it. The book is there to thrust you into life, again and again chasing you off the couch, challenging you into new adventures".[147]

God is our life coach on the most amazing run from source to sea, and every kayaker knows the need we have for great coaches. Reading his guide book can only help on the journey. As Ken Whiting encourages, "For many areas, there are guidebooks with detailed descriptions and images of rivers, and more of these are available each year. It's always a good idea to pick one of these up". [148] With many, many new translations of the Bible available each year as well, it is always a good idea to pick one of those up too. I pray you might give it a try.

---

146 Hybels, Bill, *The God You're Looking For*, p. 147
147 McLaren, Brian D., *Finding Faith*, p. 245
148 Whiting, Ken and Varette, Kevin, *Whitewater Kayaking – The Ultimate Guide*, p. 96

WE ALL NEED EDDIES

"As the deer pants for a stream of cool water, so I long for you, O God."

Psalm 42:1

*"At the lake's edge we are drawn to drag our kayaks out over the beach onto the water. We are drawn to listen to the gentle lapping of waves.
It speaks to us and we listen. We try to understand and in our still attentiveness it writes its wisdom on our souls."*

Susan Saint Sing, *Spirituality of Sport*, p. 62

"Kayaking can be quiet meditation or intense excitement, thought-provoking adventure and passionate play",[149] says Doug Ammons. This sport sure can be all these things, and it is the richer for the variety of dynamics it has to offer. Yet I happen to be writing this chapter at the end of a day when I could do with kayaking being that "quiet medita-tion". I am in need of an eddy in my life where I can stop to reflect on what has been, where I am now, and where things might be leading tomorrow.

---

149 Ammons, Doug, *Whitewater Philosophy*, p. 5

You'll have had days like this too – numerous telephone calls to make, meetings to prepare for and attend, a message from your spouse asking you to stop off and pick up some milk and bread, the children requiring dad's taxi service to one of their activities, a dental appointment to fit in and a whole host of other demands upon time and energy that just stress us out and cause us to long for peace.

I purposely wrote that last paragraph without breaking it down into more manageable sentences with the most helpful of punctuation marks: a full stop. It helpfully illustrates that we all need periods when *we* stop! Kayaking, too, needs us to come to a full stop at times, to look upstream, downstream and at the water flowing by. Even extreme kayaker Tao Berman agrees: "Typically, eddies are mini harbours . . . they allow a period of rest. . . . Eddies then, are normally a kayaker's best friend".[150] And so, in the following pages I encourage us to think about our need for rest, prayer and reflection on the metaphorical river, as well as on the literal water.

It's not for no reason that life has been likened to a river time and again. We all encounter incessant spells with rapid activity, then stretches that are more placid. Thankfully, there are beautiful calm places where the water is flat, the flow is slow and the eddies hold us still for a while. It is in such eddies that we can gather our thoughts and just take stock. The faith community has sanctioned and encouraged the importance of such places since its beginning.

When we are told that God rested on the seventh day in the creation story, there immediately was a sign that suggested time out was as important as busyness. Continuing on, the Bible encourages us to follow his lead and make space.

---

150 Berman, Tao, *Going Vertical – The Life of an Extreme Kayaker*, p. 49

"Be still and know that I am God."

Psalm 46:10

"Those who wait on the Lord shall renew their strength."

Isaiah 40:31

"Come to me all who are weary and I shall give you rest."

Matthew 11:28

Jesus used to go up a hill by himself to cope with the demands that were constantly upon him. When he taught about prayer he encouraged us to go behind closed doors, to a place of quiet and solitude, so that we can be ourselves and God can be God.

Sadly, the church, which we ordinarily think of as an oasis of calm and prayer, has become rather more of a busy voluntary organisation full of targets and hectic schedules. Many a congregation is possessed by hyper-activity with fundraising campaigns, children's ministries, men's groups, women's groups, study groups, youth groups, walking groups, reading groups. . . . Someone needs to look after property matters. Someone else needs to chair safeguarding procedures for the more vulnerable in our midst. Others need to plan worship, tidy the garden, organise visits to the housebound, raise money for the proverbial roof fund. In this hive of activity, seven days a week, the need for prayerful eddies are ever more necessary than before.

In canoe clubs it is often no different. Who's organising the pool sessions for new members? Who is in charge of security arrangements for the clubs expensive resources? Has someone arranged transport for the river trip at the weekend? What about insurance, organising a river safety course, trying out some play-boating or polo or sea kayaking sessions? Everyone has ideas but few have the time and the energy to put the ideas into practise. Life is busy. Life is demanding. Life is hard.

All of this, of course, is symptomatic of our society in general. What is it with us in our modern world when we have washing machines not washboards, fast cars instead of slow horses and carts, and yet there still never seems to be enough spare time? We are materially rich but time and spirit poor. We really do need some eddies.

The fact is that, on the actual river, you'll never cope with the constant rush of the water if you don't develop a good bow rudder that can steer you into the smallest of calm pools, which is what an eddy effectively is. Paddling over the wave trains, manoeuvring around and through the whirlpools, boofing over holes and dropping over waterfalls will eventually just fatigue us. But behind something that stops the flow, that's where we find the rest and a point of assessment that will ultimately help us along our route, safely on our way.

Ken Whiting explains, "An eddy is a pocket of water directly downstream from some form of obstruction, for example, a rock or part of the river bank that juts out. The deflection of water by the obstruction creates a relatively calm area below – a paddler's parking spot".[151]

Public worship in the church, as well as being a place of challenge, is meant to be an eddy when we need it. In fact, in his book, *Behold I do a New Thing*, Keith Hadaway has argued that, ideally, worship should be like "a raft ride down a mountain river, with exciting passages that leave us breathless and calm places where we sit and contemplate – with bends and curves where we cannot see where we are going".[152]

---

151 Whiting, Ken, *Whitewater Kayaking*, p. 99
152 Quoted in Giles, Richard, *Creating Uncommon Worship*, p. 9

Certainly, at least for one hour out of the other 167 in the week, worship can offer the general public an opportunity for prayer, praise and reflection that helps us put everything else into context. In the array of 'stuff' that flows down our river of life, in a church service we have time to stop, to think, to reflect, to contextualise, to thank, to seek help, to ponder, to pray. We may stand, sit or kneel, close our eyes or keep them open. Some might clasp, lift or open their hands and stay silent or sing out strong. But what is for sure is that, in such moments of congregational praise, our bodies and our spirits unite in a place of peace amidst the bustle. Oh, how it can feel like refreshing water to the soul.

"We are bodies as well as souls", says David Scott in his book, *Moments of Prayer*. "Our bodies can assist our prayer as much as they can distract. . . . We need to find a place on the face of the earth where we can do our praying."[153] The place I have found on the face of the earth, where I can do my praying, is actually a place on the surface of the river. Interestingly, there are others who have come before me who have found this too. Those who produce material for worship have found the inspiration of the river as inspirational as God himself. Hymns have reflected this throughout the ages.

"Like a river glorious is God's perfect peace,
Over all victorious in its bright increase;
Perfect, yet it floweth fuller every day,
Perfect, yet it groweth deeper all the way.
Stayed upon Jehovah, hearts are fully blest;
Finding as he promised, perfect peace and rest."[154]

---

153 Scott, David, *Moments of Prayer*, p. 18
154 Havergal, Frances Ridley, *Mission Praise* No. 421

These are the words of Frances Ridgley Havergal's 19th century hymn.

I'm not going to comment on them, but simply suggest we might read them over again right now, pause for a moment or two, and reflect a little as to whether there is anything in such text that is helpful to our inner self. Go on, try it. Read those words of praise once more, intentionally, purposefully, meditatively.

Now have a little read of these words:

"Like a mighty river flowing,
Like a flower in beauty growing,
Far beyond all human knowing,
Is the perfect peace of God."[155]

This more contemporary piece is by Michael Perry. Again, why not be still and reflect on whether you can relate to the rhythmic pattern of flowing, growing, knowing.

Another contemporary song is by the prolific hymnwriter, Graham Kendrick. It is known as *Shine Jesus Shine*. In this well-loved and well-worn praise item there is a line that says,

"Flow River Flow,
Flood the nations
With grace and mercy."[156]

Ponder a while. What does such imagery do for our spirits? Flood the nations with grace. Flood the nations with mercy. Flow, river, flow.

Finally, the following are the words of a traditional African American spiritual, sung by those who were bru-

155 Perry, Michael, *Mission Praise* No. 419
156 Kendrick, Graham, *Mission Praise* No. 445

tally enslaved and forced into hard labour on the cotton fields and tobacco plantations.

> *"Ol' man river,*
> *Dat ol' man river,*
> *He mus' know sumpin'*
> *But don't say nuthin'*
> *He jes' keeps rollin'*
> *He keeps on rollin' along."*

What is there in such lyrics that can help connect us to the past and to justice, and to God himself, the river giver, who is with us in our circumstances too?

I've purposely changed gear in the opening sections of this chapter and am encouraging you to do so also.

Slow down.

Don't just try to finish off reading yet another chapter in yet another book here.

Sometimes we need new patterns.

Here I'm inviting us all to slow down in order to realise that, even in the exhilaration of whitewater kayaking, there are times of peace that are crucial if we are to endure and enjoy the times of adventure and adrenalin.

Keep on coming back to the above verses and focus upon them.

Indeed, turn also to the prayers I have written in the chapter entitled "River Giver". I hope you might find them all helpful in finding your soul's eddy.

The book *Ride the River* says, "In our life journey, prayer is like gathering around the breakfast campfire, talking over the days assignments. Sitting around the evening campfire, discussing the day's happenings. Going over plans for the next day or the next week. Pulling over to the shore to take care of an emergency that has come up".[157] I like Larry Christenson's imagery here, but I'd want to add that we don't even need to be on the bank or shore. Prayer can take place right in our kayak whilst upon the water – and it often does prior to a big waterfall!!!

Prayer can take place in many an eddy, as we just take stock of where we are, where we have come from and where we need to head off to next. "The river has functioned as a barrier to freedom, a means of escape, a place of solace, source of food, and the place of baptism".[158] I want to add to this list from Archie Smith's book, *Navigating the Deep River* that the river also functions as a place of prayer.

For me, leading church worship is my job, so this public setting is not quite as much of an oasis of calm as I hope it is for others. This is why I use my kayak for some prayer time instead. Pray-boating I call it!

In the city centre of Perth, yards away from the church I serve, it is possible to paddle upstream for around half a mile. The water is flat and the current is less powerful, so I kayak against the flow in order to keep fit, working hard to gain momentum against the current on the largest river in Scotland. Usually it takes me around forty minutes to get as far as I am able, which just happens to be parallel to Scone Palace, the former crowning place of Scottish kings! The bliss comes after this when I turn the boat around, face downstream again, and lift my paddle out of the water to simply drift with the current.

During the fifteen minutes or so that it takes to get back to the point of entry, I pray, I think, I meditate and I contemplate. It's not as nerve-wracking as plunging over a waterfall or as exciting as surfing a wave, but this time on

157 Christenson, Larry, *Ride the River*, p. 127
158 Smith Jr, Archie, *Navigating the Deep River*.

the water is some of the most important time I have. There I can bring all the important matters of the day before the Source of all that is. I drop some of my worries down to the riverbed, I ask blessings on some of my loved ones, I seek assistance with some of my responsibilities and I confess my many failings. As Philip Yancey says in his book, *Prayer – Does it Make any Difference?* "I can sit silent before God, and still we can communicate – sometimes even better".[159] Usually I don't have enough time on these river trips, but it is a good start; a good proactive investment of some quality time for physical and spiritual exercise, and I guard it with a passion.

The Old Testament Prophet Isaiah spoke of the possibility of having, "Peace like a river" if we pay attention to the things God wants of us (Isaiah 48:18 / 66:12). Jesus said too that amidst all the worries we can have in this life we can know that God has not forgotten us if we "Seek first the Kingdom of God" (Matthew 6:33). Bear Grylls, the outdoor adventurer, seems to have similar feelings for such times in nature. "The natural world is", he says, "in every way, bigger, better, cleverer and stronger than us. It is only when we return to these so-called 'wilds' of nature that I find my own spirit comes alive."[160] On my times of 'prayboating' I understand what Isaiah, Jesus and Bear Grylls are talking about.

Kayakers find their spirits coming alive on the water. By sitting in the eddies of our life's river, too, we can become one with dimensions of creation other than ourselves. We remember, once more, that there are so many aspects of the river that are just like our lives, like the very things I've been addressing in this book. And in this unity, in this

---

159 Yancey, Philip, *Prayer – Does it Make Any Difference?*, p. 52
160 Grylls, Bear, *Born Survivor*, p. 8

oneness, a peace, a calm, a serenity can, and often does, descend.

Actually, we don't need to even say anything. We can just stop. We can be still. We can listen. We can look. "We have been so programmed to think of prayer as the words we say rather than something we experience with God",[161] says Jeff Imbach in *The River Within*. Why not just let you be you, the river be the river and God be God. Mentally, emotionally, spiritually the Creator and the created can become one with each other.

By observing the river's flow, and contemplating what we view, we can see with our souls, things that no one else can see. By listening to the silence all around, and contemplating what we find, we can hear with our hearts, things that no one else can hear.

In a beautiful book called *Pilgrim at Tinker Creek*, Annie Dillard writes gracefully about her time in observation of the river. "So many things have been shown me on these banks, so much light has illumined me by reflection here where the water comes down, that I can hardly believe that this grace never flags, that the pouring from ever-renewable sources is endless, impartial, and free."[162]

Again, Bear Grylls also offers a very helpful point: "You know what I think is one of the nature's greatest indulgences? The lone, hidden flower in the middle of a jungle, which no man or eye will ever see. The bloom is so crisp and clean and beautiful: it is as if such concealed wonders are God's indulgence. Made just for his pleasure".[163]

Stopping to reflect on the world around us and the world within us just can be so therapeutic – a word which comes

161 Imbach, Jeff, *The River Within*, p. 149
162 Dillard, Annie, *Pilgrim at Tinker Creek*, p. 68
163 Grylls, Bear, *Born Survivor*, p. 9

from the Greek *Therapeuo*,[164] one of the biblical words for healing. Such sentiment is contained within another quote from Annie Dillard when she declares, "Live water heals".[165] My daily work as a minister tells me very clearly that there are many in need of such therapy – not least me. I am so pleased to have found this deep connection in my recreation (read re-creation) and my occupation.

Maybe it's all just about getting perspective on things. I can accept such a thought. In fact, I was very interested to read that A. J. Jacobs, of that book I mentioned earlier, *The Year of Living Biblically,* found this to be exactly the case when he started praying without even knowing how. It's a brilliantly funny and insightful book whereby, if the Bible says do not have sex with your wife during menstruation, he keeps clear of the woman he loves. If it says eat locusts, he buys some chocolate coated ones from the internet and forces them down his throat. If it says pray – you got it – he prays. And here is what he discovered. "Day 64. A spiritual update. I'm still agnostic, but I do have some progress to report on the prayer front. I no longer dread prayer. And sometimes I'm even liking it. . . . The prayers are helpful. . . . Basically, they help me get outside of my self-obsessed cranium."[166]

When we're caught in the rapids and we're paddling and bracing and plunging and capsizing and Eskimo rolling and generally surviving, we do seldom see what is all around us. I'm not criticizing. It's just a fact. Whitewater kayaking, by definition, requires everything we have to give. The focus can become quite intense because it quite simply has to be. But eddies help us gain a wider outlook,

---

164 Vine, W.E., *Expository Dictionary of New Testament Words*, p. 203

165 Dillard, Annie, *Pilgrim at Tinker Creek*, p. 100

166 Jacobs, A.J., *The Year of Living Biblically*, pp. 94–96

a more rounded view. Why not enjoy your next eddy, not just for the rest it gives your body, but for the opportunity it can also give to nourish the soul.

It's called the practice of the presence of God – acknowledging that God is everywhere and that everywhere we are, that is where we can encounter our Source. The phrase comes from a 17th century monk called Brother Lawrence. In his book of the same title, he says, "Blind as we are we hinder God and stop the current of his graces. But when he finds a soul penetrated with a lively faith, He pours into it his graces and favours plentifully: there they flow like a torrent, which after being forcibly stopped against its ordinary course, when it has found a passage, spreads itself with impetuosity and abundance".[167]

We are often unaware of God not because God is absent but because we shut our senses off from him. Like a radio tuning into the radio waves all around, we need to tune into the Almighty's presence. Like a mobile phone, we need to find the signals that can help us communicate with the Divine.

Some might argue that they don't know how to pray. I completely understand, but would wish to reassure that there is no need to worry. As Pastor Bill Hybels has said, "The best way to learn to pray is to pray".[168] It's a bit like learning to paddle. We can learn from books, DVDs, seminars (and so we should) but we really need to take that first launch out onto the water if we really want to learn! Again and again, whilst on the water, just try to tune in. Don't, for goodness sake, close your eyes or clasp your hands! Just look around. Just gently touch the water. Just listen. Just consciously breathe in the fresh life-giving air. "Our intimacy with God will be a constant journey into

---

167 Brother Lawrence, *Practising the Presence of God*, p. 69
168 Hybels, Bill, *Too Busy Not to Pray*.

unknown territory."[169] That's exciting! One day the tiniest drops of water make their way out to sea. One day the tiniest of prayers will make their way up to heaven.

Have faith. Go where the current leads you and enjoy the eddies when they come!

169 Imbach, Jeff, *The River Within*, p. 261

LIFE IN ALL FULLNESS

"Rivers are often a route to salvation."

Bear Grylls, *Born Survivor*, p. 101

This book has been about sharing how my Christian faith and my whitewater kayaking have helped me enjoy, thus far, my life in all its possible fullness. I hope there is something – even just a quote from someone else – that might have helped you in developing your faith or in enhancing your kayaking, if you do some.

I believe, like Jeff Imbach, that "We often hold these two great desires – the longing to love God and the desire to live full, juicy lives – at arm's length, as if they are incorrigibly opposed to each other".[170] It has troubled me that some of my *kayaking* mates will think that those inside the church are just plain boring and that many of my *church* friends will think that kayaking is just plain reckless. Each group is seemingly irrelevant to one another, but it needn't be so.

Risk, capsizing, fear, adrenalin, eddies, the Source, tributaries, learning, guidebooks, living water. . . these are the things of kayaking; these are the things of faith; these are

---

170 Imbach, Jeff, *The River Within*, p. 21

the things of life. That's been my thesis. The river is an adventure. The river of life is an adventure. The river of God is an adventure. Ride it, paddle it, surf it to the full.

All I hope is that the words in these pages have taken us all at least a little further downstream to find a more interesting, exciting faith – in ourselves and in the river, and in God himself.

Life in all fullness is what I'm told Jesus came to give. I'm not prepared to settle for anything less. I hope you aren't either!

See you on the water.

See you in the church.

See you paddling the river of life.

River Giver

River giver, God of life,
I praise you and I honour you for your power and
    creativity.

You are the Source of all that is.
You provide an immense and awesome cosmos
Not a random and muddled chaos.
You lit the touch-paper of the big bang;
You encoded the data in our DNA,
You really do offer life, and life in all fullness.

Assist me to live my life to the full, enjoying the wonders
    of nature,
Not least in the dynamic waters of the creek and stream
    and burn.
As I paddle along the various stretches of life's river,
Be my companion, helping me appreciate the journey that
    I am on;
Protecting me from all harm.

I confess the times that I capsize
And the times I struggle to right myself.
I admit that I have dammed up your influence upon me.
And I acknowledge I am sometimes afraid –
    Not least of who I am,
And, sometimes, of becoming what I could yet be.

Rescue me.
Coach me.
Guide me, I ask.

Be the river of love that courses through my soul;
The river of care that overflows from my being –
With compassion and mercy, justice and love.

I will take the risk of faith.
I shall accept the challenge to trust you.
I seek, now, to fulfil the adventure of my life.

Yours are the holy, whitewaters of my re-creation.
Thank you.

AMEN

Holy Whitewater

From the Nile to the Mississippi,
From the Clyde to the Amazon,
From the Yangtze to the Thames,
Water and nourishment,
Spirituality and energy,
Pollution and waste and exploitation,
Flowing together in the river of life.
Father and Mother of Creation, forgive us when we only
  take;
Forgive us when we squander and when we desecrate
The magnificent, plentiful resources
Of your glorious creation.
Father of Creation, forgive us when we only talk;
When the flow dries up completely,
When fresh water becomes contaminated,
When fish and marine-life are threatened
In the name of "progress" and "wealth" and "power".
Forgive us, dear Lord.
Have mercy.

AMEN

In the rise and fall of tides
In the ebb and flow of life
Make me a channel of your Peace.

When I hurt from what's upstream
When I dream of what's downstream
Make me a channel of your Hope.

In the water taken from a tap
In the water shared with a stranger
Make me a channel of your Love.

When I drink in your life-giving Spirit
When I soak in your living water
Make me a channel of your Life.

In the peace of the still passage
In the angst of the rapids
Make me a channel of your presence.

When I capsize along the way
When I ignore your guidebook's wisdom
Make me a channel of your mercy.

AMEN

Holy Whitewater

From source to sea the trickle evolves
Into a cascading torrent
With wave succeeding wave,
Still water and white,
Boils and eddies and falls.
Praise God for the rivers of life.

Where we fish, where we play,
Where we wander along the bank
Where we pray,
Where otters hunt and salmon leap,
Praise God for the rivers of life.

As levels rise and fall,
As sunlight dances on reflected surface,
As liquid freezes hard,
As hardened ice melts soft once again,
Praise God for the rivers of life.

Boaters,
Fishermen,
Industry,
Community,
Pilgrims in sacred space
Soaking up the trickle and the torrent's resource,
Praise God for the rivers of life.

AMEN

Rain maker,
River Giver,
Water of our lives
I thank you for the life giving properties of H_2O.

For the refreshing and welcome drink when my throat is
   dry,
For the watering of the soil that produces rich harvest,
For the rehydration of a weary body after exertion
Thanks be to you.

Humanity needs your liquid blessing,
Wildlife and plants too.
For each drop of rain,
Each shower,
Each downpour that imparts your kindness –
Thanks be to you.

When I turn on the tap today
Let prayers of gratitude flow from my heart.
Praise you –
Rain maker,
River giver,
Holy whitewater of Life.

AMEN

BIBLIOGRAPHY

Adam, David. *The Rhythm of Life – Celtic Daily Prayer*. SPCK, London, 1996.

Ammons, Doug. *Whitewater Philosophy*. Water Nymph Press, Missoula, MT, 2009.

Armstrong, Karen. *The Bible – The Biography*. Atlantic Books, London, 2008.

Baverstock, Alison. *Is There a Book in You?* A & C Black, London 2007.

Bell, Rob. *Love Wins – At the Heart of Life's Big Questions*. HarperCollins, London, 2011.

Berman, Tao. *Going Vertical – The Life of an Extreme Kayaker*. Menasha Ridge Press, Birmingham, Alabama, 2008.

Bigelow, Jodi. *Kayaking for Fitness – An 8-Week Program to Get Fit and Have Fun*. The Heliconia Press, Ontario, 2008.

Borg, Marcus. *The Heart of Christianity*. Harper One, New York, 2003.

Bosch, David. *Transforming Mission – Paradigm Shifts in Theology of Mission*. Orbis Books, New York, 1997.

Brother Lawrence. *Practising the Presence of God*. Oneworld Publications, Oxford, 1999.

Brown, Derren. *Tricks of the Mind*. Transworld Publishers, London, 2007.

Butler, Gillian and Hope, Tony. *Manage Your Mind*. BCA, London, 1996.

Cameron, Ronald. *Tall Stories: Andy Jackson a Biography*, Pesda Press, Gwynedd, 2008.

Chalke, Steve and Mann, Alan. *The Lost Message of Jesus*. Zondervan, Grand Rapids, 2003.

Christenson, Larry. *Ride the River*. Bethany House, Minnesota, 2000.

Coffey, Maria. *Explorers of the Infinite*. The Penguin Group, London, 2008.

Collins, Francis. *The Language of God*. Pocket Books, London, 2007.

Dawkins, Richard. *The God Delusion*. Transworld Publishers, London, 2007.

Dickert, Wayne. *Basic Kayaking, All the Skills and Gear You Need to Get Started*. Stackpole Books, Mechanicsburg, 2005.

Dillard, Annie. *Pilgrim at Tinker Creek*. Harper & Row Publishers, New York, 1988.

Drane, John. *The Bible: Fact or Fantasy?* Lion Publishing, Oxford, 1990.

Drummond, Fred. *All That Jazz – Learning to Hear the Kingdom Tune in a New Setting*. Authentic Media, Milton Keynes, 2007.

Ferguson, Sinclair B. and Wright, David W. *New Dictionary of Theology*. Inter-Varsity Press, Leicester, 1993.

Ferrero, Franco. *White Water Safety & Rescue*. Pesda Press, Gwynedd, 2008.

Finley, Donny. *Peace Like a River – Refreshing Your Soul in Quiet Places*. Harvest House Publishers, Oregon, 2001.

Foster, Richard. *Prayer – Finding the Heart's True Home*. Hodder & Stoughton, London, 1992.

Fox, Matthew. *One River, Many Wells – Wisdom Springing from Global Faiths*. Penguin Group, New York, 2004.

Gardner, Dan. *Risk – The Science and Politics of Fear*. Virgin Books, London, 2009.

Gibbs, Eddie and Bolger, Ryan K. *Emerging Churches – Creating Christian Community in Postmodern Culture*. SPCK, London, 2006.

Giles, Richard. *Creating Uncommon Worship – Transforming the Liturgy of the Eucharist*. Canterbury Press, Norwich, 2004.

Grylls, Bear. *Born Survivor – Survival Techniques from the Most Dangerous Places on Earth*. Transworld Publishers, London, 2007.

Hybels, Bill. *Too Busy Not to Pray – Slowing Down to be with God*. Inter-Varsity Press, Leicester, 1994.

Hybels, Bill. *The God You're Looking For*. Thomas Nelson Publishers, London, 1997.

Imbach, Jeff. *The River Within – Loving God, Living Passionately*. Navpress, Colorado Springs, 1998.

Jacobs, A.J. *The Year of Living Biblically – One Man's Quest to Follow the Bible as Literally as Possible*. Simon and Schuster, New York, 2007.

Jones, Alan. *Reimagining Christianity – Reconnect Your Spirit Without Disconnecting Your Mind*. John Wiley & Sons, New Jersey, 2005.

Jones, Griff Rhys. *Rivers – A Voyage into the Heart of Britain*. Hodder & Stoughton, London, 2009.

King, Martin Luther, Jr. *Strength to Love*. Fount Paperbacks, 1983.

McGrath, Alister. *Christian Theology – An Introduction*. Blackwell, Oxford, 1994.

McGrath, Alister and Collicut McGrath, Joanna. *The Dawkins Delusion – Atheist Fundamentalism and the Denial of the Divine*. Society for Promoting Christian Knowledge, London, 2007.

McLaren, Brian D. and Campolo, Tony. *Adventures in Missing the Point – How the Culture-Controlled Church Neutered the Gospel*. Zondervan, Grand Rapids, 2003.

McLaren, Brian D. *A Generous Orthodoxy*. Zondervan, Grand Rapids, 2004.

McLaren, Brian D. *Finding Faith*. Zondervan, Grand Rapids, 1996.

McLaren, Brian D. *More Ready Than You Realise – Evangelism as Dance in the Postmodern Matrix*. Zondervan, Grand Rapids, 2002.

McLaren, Brian D. *The Church on the Other Side*. Zondervan, Grand Rapids, 2000.

Maxwell, John C. *Failing Forward – Turning Mistakes into Stepping Stones for Success*. Thomas Nelson Publishers, Nashville, Tennessee, 2000.

Mission Praise. Marshall Pickering, London, 1990.

Moltmann, Jurgen. *Experiences of God*. SCM Press, London, 1980.

Neil, William. *The Plain Man Looks at the Bible*. Fontana Books, London, 1974.

Neilson, Peter. *Church on the Move – New Church, New Generation, New Scotland*. Covenanters Press, Glasgow, 2005.

Ortberg, John. *If you Want to Walk on Water You've Got to Get Out of the Boat*. Christian Book Club, Devon, 2001.

Ortberg, John. *When the Game is Over it All Goes Back in the Box*. Zondervan, Grand Rapids, 2007.

Packer, James I. *Concise Theology – A Guide to Historic Christian Beliefs*. Tyndale House Publishers, Wheaton, 1993.

Partington, Angela (Ed). *The Oxford Library of Words and Phrases. Volume I: Quotations*, 2nd Edition. Oxford University Press, Oxford, 1988.

Peck Scott M. *The Road Less Travelled*. Century Hutchinson, London, 1988.

Peterson, Eugene. *The Journey – A Guidebook for the Christian Life*. Marshall Pickering, London, 1995.

Radcliffe, Timothy O.P. *What is the Point of Being a Christian?* Burns and Oates, London, 2006.

Reid, Harry. *Outside Verdict – An Old Kirk in a New Scotland.* Saint Andrew Press, Edinburgh, 2002.

Richardson, Ronald W. *Creating a Healthier Church Family Systems Theory, Leadership and Congregational Life.* Fortress Press, Minneapolis, 1996.

Riddell, Mike. *God's Homepage – A Journey Through the Bible for Postmodern Pilgrims.* The Bible reading Fellowship, Oxford, 1998.

Robertson, David. *The Dawkins Letters – Challenging Atheist Myths.* Christian Focus Publications, Ross-shire, 2007.

Robinson, Gene. *In the Eye of the Storm.* Canterbury Press, Norwich, 2008.

Saint Sing, Susan. *Spirituality of Sport – Balancing Body and Soul.* St. Anthony Messenger Press, Cincinnati, 2004.

Scott, David. *Moments of Prayer.* SPCK, London, 1997.

Simpson, J.A. *There is a Time to . . .* The Camelot Press, London, 1971.

Smith Jr, Archie. *Navigating the Deep River – Spirituality in African American Families.* United Church Press, Cleveland, Ohio, 1997.

Stott, John. *The Contemporary Christian.* Inter-Varsity Press, Leicester, 1992.

St John of the Cross. *The Dark Night of the Soul.* Hodder & Stoughton, London, 1997.

Sweet, Leonard. *Summoned to Lead.* Zondervan, Grand Rapids, 2004.

Sweet, Leonard. *Soul Tsunami – Sink or Swim in New Millennium Culture.* Zondervan, Grand Rapids, 1999.

Tejada-Flores, Lito. *Wildwater – The Sierra Club Guide to Kayaking and Whitewater Boating.* Sierra Club Books, San Francisco, 1978.

Thomas à Kempis, *The Imitation of Christ*. Penguin, Harmondsworth, 1979.

Thomas, Bridget (Ed). *Scottish Whitewater*. Pesda Press, Gwynedd, 2004.

Thornton, Martin. *The Rock and the River – An Encounter between Traditional Spirituality and Modern Thought*. Hodder & Stoughton, London, 1965.

Tidball, Derek and Hilborn, David (Eds). *The Atonement Debate – Papers from the London Symposium on the Theology of the Atonement*. Zondervan, Grand Rapids, 2008.

Vine, W.E. *Expository Dictionary of New Testament Words*. Oliphants Ltd, London, 1966.

Wallis, Jim. *The Call to Conversion*. Monarch Books, Oxford, 2006.

Warren, Rick. *Bible Study Methods – Twelve Ways You Can Unlock God's Word*. Zondervan, Grand Rapids, 2006.

Whiting, Ken and Varette, Kevin. *Whitewater Kayaking – The Ultimate Guide*. The Heliconia Press, Ontario, 2008.

White, Ruth. *Your Spiritual Journey – A Guide to the River of Life*. Judy Piatkus Publishers, London, 1999.

Wooden, John and Jamison, Steve. *Wooden on Leadership*. McGraw-Hill, New York, 2005.

Wright, Nigel. *The Radical Evangelical – Seeking a Place to Stand*. SPCK, London, 1996.

Yancey, Philip. *Prayer – Does it Make Any Difference?* Hodder & Stoughton, London, 2008.

ABOUT THE AUTHOR

Scott Burton was born in the city of Glasgow where he was formerly a plasterer in the building trade. Having studied as an adult student at the universities of St. Andrews and Aberdeen, he is now a minister in the Church of Scotland, ordained on his 30th birthday in 1999. In 2007 he was inducted to his current post of St. Matthew's Church, Perth, on the bank of the River Tay. It was at this point he fell in love with the hobby of whitewater kayaking. He is the chairman of Perth Canoe Club.

Scott is married to Jill, has two daughters, Eilidh and Sara, and a Weimaraner dog called Sophie. The Burton family, apart from Sophie, regularly enjoy international pulpit exchange experiences in the Presbyterian Church (USA). Marion, South Carolina, Los Angeles, California and Amelia Island, Florida have all enjoyed his preaching since 2005.

This is Scott's first book, all proceeds going to ministerial projects embarked upon by his congregation.